# TABLE AND BAR

**A Guide to Alcoholic Beverages, Sales and Service**

# TABLE AND BAR

## A Guide to Alcoholic Beverages, Sales and Service

Jeffrey T. Clarke

Hodder & Stoughton

A MEMBER OF THE HODDER HEADLINE GROUP

*British Library Cataloguing in Publication Data*

Clarke, Jeffrey T.
  Table and bar: a guide to
  alcoholic beverages
  1. Alcoholic beverages
  I. Title
  641.8'74

ISBN 0 7131 7511 7

First published 1987
Impression number 15 14 13 12 11 10 9 8 7 6
Year 1999 1998 1997 1996 1995 1994

Typeset by Mathematical Composition Setters Ltd.
Printed in Great Britain for Hodder & Stoughton Educational, a division of
Hodder Headline Plc, 338 Euston Road, London NW1 3BH
by J. W. Arrowsmith Ltd, Bristol.

# Contents

# Foreword

It comes as no surprise to me that Jeffrey Clarke has produced a book which is a goldmine of information on every aspect of the sale and service of alcoholic beverages because his experience in and dedication to the subject are renowned.

A wealth of knowledge and advice is presented in a clear and lively style. All the facts and figures that students and professionals need to have at their fingertips are here: how to lift a box without straining your back; what is the correct tool to use when emptying a bar ashtray (it's a 4 cm paintbrush); what height the ceiling in a pub cellar should be; what glass you should serve a Brontë in; what a puncheon is; and so on. The text is brought alive by interesting snippets of information such as that only *female* hops flower, Eton boys were flogged for *not* smoking during the Great Plague in 1665, fresh flowers are unacceptable on bar tops because earwigs might drop off into customers' glasses, and Geneva gin is so called because Geneva is the Dutch word for juniper.

I feel I now have a much clearer idea than before as to why some hotels, restaurants, pubs and bars have more efficient staff than others, making their establishments a pleasure to visit.


Patrick Forbes
Managing Director of Moët & Chandon (London) Ltd
Author of *Champagne: the wine, the land and the people*

# Preface

*Table and Bar* has been written to provide students of Alcoholic Beverages courses with a comprehensive framework of information and guidance. It is organised to make the subject-matter as readable and easy to learn as possible. This is particularly important in the early stages of a course when a student has to cope with a vast amount of new information.

There are many books published on the subject of wine and the conflicting opinions in them can often confuse the beginner. The approach in *Table and Bar* is different in that it presents not only the important information on wine but also a study of the work involved in the preparation, storage, and service of beers, spirits, liqueurs and cocktails.

The book follows syllabus requirements of City and Guilds 717 Alcoholic Beverages, Sales and Service very closely and it also presents the required background information for City and Guilds 700 Bar and Cellar programmes. It will be found suitable for students on courses leading to BTEC First Diploma and National Diploma Food and Beverage units. Much of the information included would be useful to students preparing for the examinations of the Wine and Spirit Education Trust Ltd. The book will also be of interest to anyone already involved in the industry, either as an innkeeper or hotelier.

Already over two million people are employed in hospitality outlets and catering, and this number is growing. Public interest in wines, and more recently in cocktails, has been awakened, and there are good career prospects for those who have the necessary skills and knowledge. Opportunities for travel are increasing, as the language of alcoholic beverages is international, and training and qualifications gained in the UK are recognised world-wide. Finally, my colleagues and friends in the Guild of Sommeliers and the United Kingdom Bartenders' Guild would agree with me that there is great pleasure and satisfaction to be gained from working in this sector of the industry.


Jeffrey T. Clarke

# Acknowledgements

The publishers would like to thank the following for their permission to reproduce copyright material and illustrations:

Dopff p24;
The Guild of Sommeliers and Geoffrey Mowbray Ltd p3;
Hotel Catering and Institutional Management Association p3;
R & C Vintners p49;
Sharp Electronics (UK) Ltd and MCC Public Relations Ltd p155;
Wine and Spirit Education Trust Ltd p3;
Moët & Chandon (London) Ltd p16;
Andrew Durkan p27 top;
Gonzalez Byass (UK) Ltd p79;
M. K. Refrigeration Ltd p92;
Noviss-Coachhouse Ltd p110;
Whitbread & Co plc .Sheffield Press Pictures p115;
ICI Plant Protection Division p119;
George H. Hall p120;
Mansell Collection Ltd pp129 left & right and 134;
Wine & Spirit Magazine (the Evro Publishing Company) p153;
Sharp Electronics (UK) Ltd p55 left & right;
Chubb Fire Security Ltd pp171 top & bottom (Chorley Hyman & Rose), 172 top (David A. Hare) & bottom, 173 top & bottom (David A. Hare), 174 top right & left (both Chorley Hyman & Rose);
Ellis Mechanical Services Ltd p174 bottom.
The photographs on pp54, 55, 56, 57, 58, 59, 60, 61, 62, 64, 72, 73, 93, 97, 101, 105, 108, 109 bottom, 112, 113, 114, 124, 141 and 143 were supplied by Julian Clarke.

The author would like to thank the following for all their help: S. Hewitt, Head of Department of Catering, Worcester Technical College; Mr and Mrs Cross, Talbot Hotel, Barbourne, Worcester; Giffard Hotel, Worcester; The Old Swan Brewery, Cheltenham; Whitbread Flowers and Co., Cellar Services, Gloucester; Bulmers Cider, Worcester.

# Part 1:

# A Service Industry

*The Industry*
*Alcohol Sales Outlets*

# The Industry

The hotel, catering and leisure industries are made up of a wide variety of different units and groups. Some of them are not concerned with the sale or service of alcohol, and some of them are not governed by the profit motive, but together they contribute to the national economy by:

a) providing employment for over two million people, directly in the provision of food, drink, and accommodation, and indirectly in the many, many more who work in the manufacture of the goods sold through the industry, and the furnishings, fittings and equipment used;
b) generating the tourist flow from abroad and also within the UK; and
c) amassing large amounts of money paid to the Inland Revenue, by way of income tax, the VAT Collectors for services and goods sold, and the Customs and Excise Department in respect of duties paid on beers, wines, spirits, and tobacco imported into the country or manufactured at home.

*Hotels* may be privately-owned individual units, or links in a national or international chain. They range from *bed and breakfast* houses to plushly appointed *luxury* establishments. Brewery companies maintain and run the majority of the *public houses* in Britain. Each 'pub' has its own character, developed by the licensee and his team, and provides food, drink and entertainment for locals and for travellers. The British pub has no equal anywhere in the world.

*Restaurants* providing *speciality foods* are numerous. Among the most successful are those offering Chinese and Indian cuisines. *Fast-food* outlets concentrate mainly on one food, such as pizzas, hamburgers, doughnuts, etc. *Wine bars* and *cocktail bars* are fashionable and popular venues, offering new and varied drink experiences; they have benefited from the increasing interest in wines and cocktails which has developed over the last decade. *Conference* and *banquet* facilities cater for very large groups, often from business and political organisations. It is becoming more and more common for *leisure complexes* and *sports centres* to include bars and eating areas in the list of facilities they provide.

*Private clubs,* offering catering and bar arrangements, and sometimes live entertainment, attract large paid memberships. *Contract catering* businesses have been set up to take on the day-to-day requirements of factories, schools, hospitals, etc., and provide the necessary specialist experience to respond to the needs of the management. *University* and *college* catering units often provide conference and holiday facilities during the vacations when residential students are absent.

*Industrial catering* is a very large sector which specialises in round-the-clock provision of meals for management and workers, in very large numbers and in a limited time. *Hospital* and *welfare* catering is concerned with the provision of food and drink to those who are not in a position to choose where or what they will eat or drink. Many of the customers may require special diets. *Prison* caterers serve a captive clientele.

*Transport* catering enterprises wine and dine people as they travel.

*Rail fare* provides dining and buffet car facilities for British Rail. *Flight* catering has to adapt to rapidly changing time scales and the eating traditions of different nationalities. *Liners* on world cruises must plan their storage and replenishment of foodstuffs with great care. *Motorway* service areas provide a variety of food services for fast-moving non-regular customers.

The *Armed Forces* cater for very large numbers of personnel, often in conditions where the rations have to be carried on the backs of the men and women themselves. The logistics of food and drink provision are planned to cover any eventuality.

## Professional and technical associations

**HCIMA** (Hotel Catering and Institutional Management Association) This organisation is the professional association for managers and potential managers in every sector of the catering and accommodation services industry. Entry requirements include both specific qualifications and on-the-job experience. The range of membership grades, from student to fellowship, is designed to suit applicants at every stage of career development.

Address: 191 Trinity Road, London SW17 7HN.

**UKBG** (United Kingdom Bartender's Guild) This Guild is open to suitably trained bartenders who work regularly in bars. Student membership is encouraged. Each new member has to be proposed by someone who is already a member. A bi-monthly magazine is published.

Address: 91–93 Gordon Road, Harbourne, Birmingham B17 9HA.

**Guild of Sommeliers** The world's most famous organisation of wine butlers, this Guild has links with other similar organisations abroad. Student members are welcomed. The Guild organises visits and promotes and organises educational courses, including the annual Sommelier of the Year competition. A monthly magazine is sent to all members.

Address: 30 Birdhurst Rise, South Croydon, Surrey CR2 7ED.

**Licensed Victuallers Association** Every town, city or country region has a branch of this organisation which works for the licensees in its area, and mobilises support in the interests of the trade in general.

**Brewer's Society** This association of brewers was formed to co-ordinate the promotion and development of publicity and research with a view to encouraging efficient cellar and public-house management.

Address: 42 Portman Square, London W1.

**Wine and Spirit Education Trust Ltd** This educational body was set up by the Wine and Spirit Association of Great Britain to develop educational courses for the wine trade. The Certificate, Higher Certificate, and Diploma courses are available at several centres.

Address: Five Kings House, Kennet Wharf Lane, Upper Thames St, London EC4V 3BE.

# Alcohol Sales Outlets

There are more than 168 000 outlets licensed to sell alcohol in the UK. This figure can be broken down as follows:

| | |
|---|---|
| Full licences (pubs and hotels) | 75 000 |
| Restaurant and residential licences | 20 000 |
| Licensed clubs | 32 000 |
| Off-licences | 41 000 |

The sales emphasis will be different in each type of outlet. In bars, for example, the best seller is draught beer, followed by bottled beers, spirits, aperitifs, cocktails, wine, and finally liqueurs. In restaurants the popularity is almost reversed, with wine topping the list followed by aperitifs, liqueurs, spirits, cocktails, bottled beers, and draught beer. For off-licences, where alcohol can only be bought in closed vessels, the sales preference is as follows: wine, aperitifs, spirits, bottled beers, and liqueurs.

## Free trade

A *free house* is a privately-owned public house or licensed hotel with no tie to any brewery. The manager can purchase his beer, wines and spirits freely from any source he chooses. The profits from sales belong to the owner.

## Tenancies

A *tenant* licensee controls the running of a public house or licensed hotel which belongs to a brewer or a large company. It is usual for him to pay an 'ingoing' which usually amounts to several thousand pounds and rent for the premises, the rate of which is reviewed after a fixed period of years. The tenant manages his own business and may be responsible for repairs and general upkeep of the premises, but is expected to purchase his beer from the parent company.

## Management

A brewery may own the licensed house and appoint a manager or managers (often a husband and wife team). They are paid a salary and must expect to move to another property if the brewery requires them to do so.

Over the last twenty years the licensed trade has changed and has acquired a completely new image. Many millions of pounds are being spent by the brewers to improve the appeal of the 'local' in the face of competition from many quarters. Main causes for concern include a disturbing 84 per cent increase in the number of off-licences, and the ever-increasing popularity of wine bars and clubs, many of which are able to remain open after the pub has closed. Other contributory factors include: a 25 per cent decline in the amount of beer consumed in the UK; drink/driving legislation; a boom in home videos and computers; home brewing; unemployment; and high duty rates.

# Part 2:

# Wine From Many Countries

# Definitions

## What is wine?

Wine is the alcoholic beverage obtained from the fermentation of the juice of freshly gathered grapes, a process which has been carried out in the district of origin and according to local practice and tradition.

## Colour of wine

*Red* wine is made from *black* grapes. The colour pigment in the skins of the black grape is an 'indicator' which turns red in the presence of acid (in the juice). The black skins are left in the fermentation.

*Rosé:* the skins of the black grape are left in the fermentation for between 24 and 36 hours so that some of the red colour is retained.

*White* wine can be made from any colour of grape. When a white wine is required from black grapes, as in champagne, the skins must be removed as soon as the pressing is complete.

## Sweetness in wine

*Dry wine* results from all the sugar having been consumed by the yeast.

*Sweet wine* results when sugar remains in the wine after the yeast has died.

*Table wine* is the result of the natural fermentation of grape juice.

*Tonic wines* are table wines which have had vitamins and/or health improvers added to them (e.g. Wincarnis contains beef extract).

*Fortified wines* are table wines to which has been added grape spirit (brandy) to bring the alcoholic strength up to approximately 20 per cent. The brandy may be added during fermentation, as in port wine, or after fermentation, as in sherry.

*Sparkling wine* is made when the carbon dioxide gas ($CO_2$), which is produced during fermentation, is imprisoned in the wine and not allowed to escape. The trapped gas is the result of a secondary fermentation either in the bottle, as in champagne, or in large sealed tanks. (In the making of non-sparkling wine, the gas is allowed to escape from the top of the cask, vat or tank.)

## Vintage

This word literally means 'harvest'. The wines of a particularly good year are referred to as 'vintage wines', and are usually the product of a very fine year. Some excellent years have been 1927, 1945, 1957, 1959, 1961, 1964, 1970, 1976, 1978, 1983 and 1985. The year 1963 was generally very poor, although it was good for port. Vintages do, of course, vary according to areas.

*Non-vintage* wines are a blend of wine of different years.

*Aperitifs* are alcoholic beverages which are drunk before the meal.

*Digestifs* are drinks consumed after the meal.

# Vine-growing Latitudes

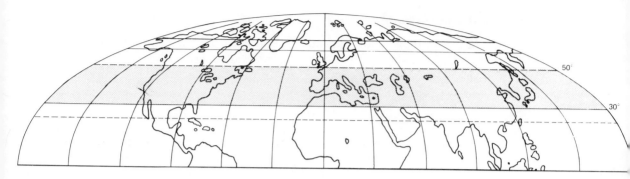

*The northern hemisphere*

The wine-producing countries of the world all lie in two belts around the earth, where the climate is neither too cold nor too hot for the cultivation of the vine. The lines of latitude which mark the two extremes of temperature variation are *30°* and *50°* in both the Northern and the Southern hemispheres. The south of England is on the very edge of the cold northern limit of vine production.

*Europe* is ideally situated for wine growing and produces three-quarters of the world's wine. *France* produces more fine wine than any other country and *Italy* and *France together* produce more than one-half of all the wine drunk in the world. *Italy* is regarded as the world's largest producer, closely followed by France. Germany produces wines of very fine quality but the quantity is small (less than Bordeaux). For various reasons not all areas of the world which are ideally situated to grow the vine, and make wine, do so to any great extent. *New Zealand,* for example, is very well placed but has only a small wine industry.

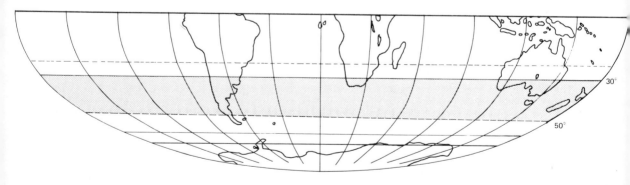

*The southern hemisphere*

# Factors influencing the Character of Wine

## Soil

It has wrongly been suggested that the vine will only grow in poor soil. The truth is that vines will grow in any type of soil and have the capacity to thrive where most other crops would find existence impossible.

Much of the nature of wine is derived from the composition of the soil, especially in relation to its acidity and mineral make-up.

## Grape variety

Over 5000 varieties of vine exist, but only just over one hundred are used by the wine-makers of Europe. Each variety has its own individual flavour and bouquet. The Pinot Noir and Cabernet Sauvignon are fine quality black grapes, and the Riesling and Chardonnay are white.

## Latitude

Wine made nearer the 30° lines of latitude, where the mean temperature is much higher, will tend to be of a lower quality than those near the 50° lines. Fermentation will be fast and the resulting wine will probably be bland and uninteresting.

## Climate

Frost, wind, rain, hail and sunshine each in their own way contribute, for good or ill, to the character of wine (see Viticulture, page 10).

## Aspect

Vines grown on south-facing slopes will usually make finer wine, due to longer exposure to the sunshine. Northerly aspects do not have the same advantages and vines grown there are less likely to produce good wine.

## Viticulture

Care and cultivation of the vine, so as to produce the best possible wine, has become a highly technical industry in some areas. Ploughing, pruning, weeding, spraying and harvesting all have their place on the vineyard calendar and each can affect the resulting wine.

## Vinification

Every wine-maker approaches his or her task in an individual way and determines the level of technology that will be used in the production of his or her wines.

## Age

Wines are like people: they develop, mature, sometimes become sick, and finally deteriorate with age, and die. Wines of certain years have a longer lifespan. The flavour of wine changes as it matures with age.

# Viticulture

All the classical varieties of grape-vine grown in Europe belong to the species *Vitis vinifera*. They produce, when carefully tended, wines of great distinction. They are, however, prone to attack from a small grub which destroys the roots. This grub develops into the aphid *phylloxera vastatrix* which was first discovered on vines in England in 1858 and went on to devastate the vineyards of Europe and many other parts of the world before a remedy was discovered. The ravages of the grub were brought under control by the end of the century by *grafting* the European vine onto American rootstock which was found to be resistant to phylloxera.

Grafting in warm climates can be done onto the growing root, in situ, but in cold northern vineyards the graft is effected in peat-boxes in hot-houses.

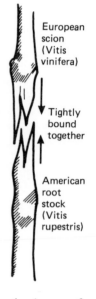

European scion (Vitis vinifera)

Tightly bound together

American root stock (Vitis rupestris)

*A vine graft*

### Work in the vineyards

In the Northern hemisphere, winter pruning usually starts after *St Vincent's day* (22 January). During the cold season, frost is welcomed as it helps to kill some disease organisms, but if the temperature falls below $-15°C$ the plant will die. Desperate measures must be taken to protect the vine. Smudge pots of oily rags are lit and the soil is earthed-up around the base of the vine. In *March*, stakes and wires are renewed and strengthened. New grafted vines are planted out.

In most regions the expected production life of each vine is about thirty years. In its first four years it is not mature enough to make good wine.

In *April* the soil is taken away from the base of the plant to aerate the soil and to collect the spring rains. Frost is unlikely, but if it occurs it will be disastrous to the buds. In *May* the vines are dusted with sulphur to prevent *Oidium*. Flowering takes place in *late May or June* and warm still days are required for pollination to take place.

Weeds must be continually removed throughout the season. In *June* and *July* sprays of *copper sulphate* are used to prevent *black-rot* and *downy mildew* and summer pruning is carried out. In *August* sulphuring continues until five weeks before the vintage, which starts in *September*. Warm sunny weather is needed to ripen the fruit. In some areas the grower may leave his fruits even until into *November* or *December* to ripen and wither. *Botrytis cinerea* or 'noble rot', which may develop, provides wine which is very sweet and also expensive (e.g. Sauternes). After the vintage, time is spent in ploughing, manuring, and tidying up the vineyard.

In the Southern hemisphere the various activities take place at the opposite time of year.

*Note* Methods of pruning differ according to the district.

# Vinification of Table Wine

It is important that the wine-making process is started as soon as possible after the harvest. Each vigneron in his own district makes wine in his own particular way, usually after the fashion of his forefathers.

The grapes are pressed in a number of different ways, the old foot-pressing method being used only in remote mountain districts now. *Hydraulic* and *Archimedean screw* presses are popular in some regions, while others use the *revolving cylinder* or the *pneumatic bar* press. This last is like a large balloon inside a cylinder. The balloon is placed amongst the grapes and then inflated, forcing the juice out through the slatted sides.

If the wine-maker is producing wine intended for early drinking, the stalks are removed in a machine which the French call a *foulloir-egrappoire*. The resulting wine will be low in *tannin*, the natural chemical in grape stalks which gives wine its keeping quality. Beaujolais Nouveau is one of the wines made in this way.

The colour of wine comes from the grapeskins. So if a white wine is to be made from red grapes, the juice must be separated from the skins immediately after pressing, Juice for rosé wine is left in contact for a short time, approximately one day (24 hours).

Fermentation is the conversion of *natural sugars* (or *added sugars* in poor years when the authorities permit), into *carbon dioxide gas* and *alcohol,* by the action of *yeast.* The yeast may be found on the outside of the grapeskins, but many areas use a pure culture of yeast cultivated in laboratories.

Ideally the process will be completed in approximately four weeks. But in hot climates fermentation may be over in a week, whereas in colder regions it sometimes takes several months.

Wine-makers in many districts prefer wooden casks for the fermentation of their wine, especially the red wines, followed by several years of maturation in oak. Sediment will form in the casks during the maturation and it is necessary to *rack* the wine into clean casks, to separate it from the sediment, twice each year.

Evaporation occurs during the wine's life in cask. The space must be topped up with similar wine to exclude the air and therefore prevent deterioration. Alternative vessels used in wineries include stainless steel containers, concrete vats, and glass fibre tanks.

*Sulphur dioxide* is used to control the fermentation process. It is added early, just after the first signs of activity are seen, and its purpose is to eliminate the harmful wild yeasts and the vinegar-forming *acetobacter.* During maturation the sulphur taste disappears.

*Blending* may take place before the wine is sold in order to achieve the most acceptable and saleable product. Wines which are too acidic may be blended with rounder, fuller wines to satisfy the consumer's palate.

11

# French Wine and Spirit Areas

**Alsace**   The vines are grown on the eastern slopes of the *Vosges* mountains, the vineyards are on the French side of the border with Germany. Wines produced are mainly dry white and are labelled after the variety of grape used.

**Armagnac**   A fine earthy brandy, comparable with cognac.

**Burgundy North**   The area is known as the 'Côte d'Or'. Exceptionally fine red wines in the Côte de Nuits in the north and superb red and white wines in the Côte de Beaune.

**Burgundy South**   This area produces good red and white wines in the Mâconnais, and popular light red wines in Beaujolais in the south.

**Bordeaux**   An area noted mainly for excellent red wines known as claret, and world-renowned sweet white wines. Some dry white wines are produced in Entre-deux-mers.

**Calvados**   Spirit produced from apples and pears in Normandy.

**Chablis**   Excellent dry white wine. The area is north-west of Burgundy and the wines are similar to the Côte de Beaune whites.

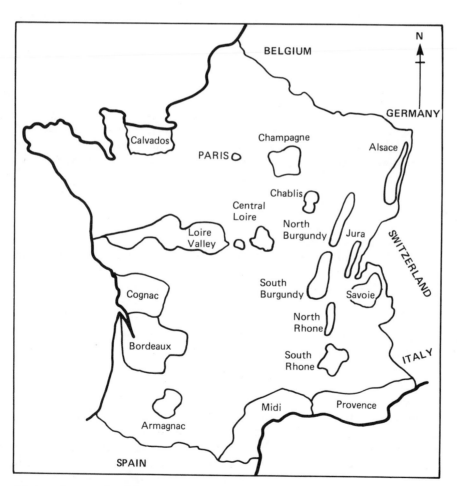

*Main wine and spirit areas*

**Champagne.** The world's finest celebration wine. It is made in a restricted area of France, by secondary fermentation in the bottle.

**Central Loire**   Very fine dry white wines produced in vineyards more than 300 miles from the coast.

**Cognac**   Undoubtedly the world's most distinguished brandy.

**Jura**   Many varieties of wine are produced in this area of eastern France near the borders of Switzerland.

**Loire**   Fine quality dry and sweet white wines, delightful rosés, sparkling wines made by the same method as champagne, and some red wines of great character, are examples of the wide variety of wines from the 'Garden of France'.

**Midi**   Produces large quantities of wines of average quality. The French vermouth trade is centred in this area. Some fine VDQS wines.

**Provence**   Average quality wines are produced from extensive vineyard areas. Good, sound wines of all types, including VDQS, and AOC.

**Rhône North**   Steeply terraced area with high quality AOC wines, both red and white. Wines high in alcohol.

**Rhône South**   Rolling hillsides producing fine AOC wines. Due to maximum sunshine, the red, white, and rosé wines are full-bodied and rich in alcohol. Some VDN (fortified) wines.

**Savoie**   'Local' wines of average quality. Some good dry white wines and fair quality reds. Some sparkling wines are also produced.

# Champagne

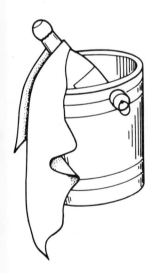

This celebration wine originated from the district of Champagne, the most northerly French wine area. It is made in a small and restricted corner of France and has no equal in the world. It is the symbol of success and achievement.

The quality of champagne is largely due to the great depth of *chalk soil* which, in the better vineyards, is covered with a thin layer of rich, dark top-soil.

The three classic grape varieties used in the area are the black *Pinot Noir* and *Pinot Meunier,* which make up about 75 per cent of the final blend, and the white *Chardonnay.* A small amount of pink (rosé) champagne is made. It is interesting to note that although the main production is a beautifully crystal-clear sparkling white wine, it is made up of grapes which are mostly black. The freshly pressed juice is separated from the skins immediately upon pressing, so that no colour is taken from the skins. The pink champagne is made by adding a little red wine, from the village of Bouzy, later in the process.

### Dom Pérignon

Dom Pérignon (1638–1715) was a monk, and cellarer, at the Abbey of *Hautvillers.* He was responsible for the finances of the abbey and also the purchases of food and wine. He developed what we now know as champagne by carrying out experiments in clarification and sparkle in wine. He also re-introduced the cork.

## Swizzle-sticks (or mossers)

In Victorian times the bubbles were sometimes stirred out of champagne using a swizzle-stick. They were made from silver or gold, with a much cheaper one made of wood for lesser folk.

## Keeping quality

It takes between three and seven years to produce a bottle of champagne. Non-vintages should be drunk within two or three years of purchase; if stored correctly, vintage champagnes of a great year sometimes remain in excellent drinking condition for a decade or longer.

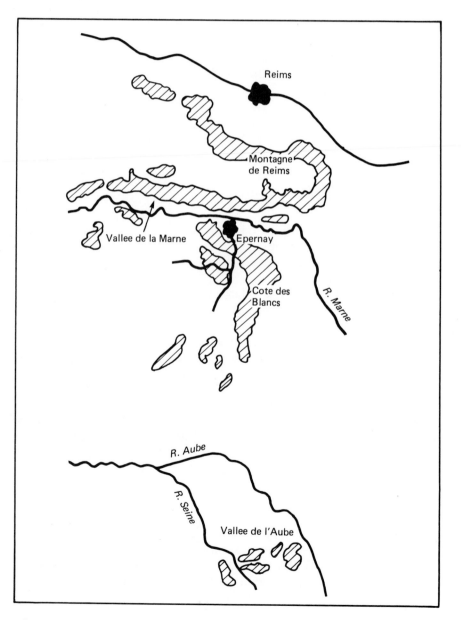

The chalk soil of champagne, now nearly 2000 feet above sea-level, was once the sea-bed. It is hard to imagine that ocean creatures inhabited those fruitful areas which now produce the most remarkable drink experience ever. The white Chardonnay grapes are concentrated in the area known as the *Côte des Blancs* (literally 'slope of whites') south of *Epernay*. The *Montagne de Reims*, the *Vallée de la Marne*, and the *Vallée de l'Aube* complete the districts of Champagne. There are more than 250 villages whose wines are blended by the 26 *Grande Marque* houses of international repute. Names like *Moët & Chandon, Krug, Mumm & Co, Veuve Clicquot, Charles Heidseick, Pol Roger*, and *Lanson*, etc., make up the champagne stage. Most of the growers are owners of small parcels of land and they sell their grapes annually, by seasonal arrangement, to the shippers, thus ensuring that even if the season was a disaster they would not suffer too great a financial hardship.

### Méthode champenoise

Champagne is made in the following manner, the whole process taking approximately five years.

1. **Pressing**   4000 kilos of grapes. This is called the *marc*.
   1st pressing—*Ten* casks of *Vin de Cuvée* (2000 litres).
   2nd pressing—*Two* casks of *Première Taille* (444 litres)
   3rd pressing—*One* cask of *Deuxième Taille* (222 litres)
   4th pressing—*One* cask of *Rebêche*. This last cask is of much lower quality and must not be sold as champagne.
2. **First fermentation**   This takes place in the cask. Fermentation starts about eight hours after pressing. The result is a *still dry* white wine. This wine is left in the cask for *five* months, when it is *racked* (put into new casks) and *fined* (clarified).
3. **Assemblage**   This is the blending together of the wines of any number of the 250 different village wines produced in the region.
4. **Yeast and cane sugar**, in wine solution, is added. (This solution is known as *liqueur de tirage.*)
5. **Bottling**   The wine is bottled and the bottles are then *mis sur lattes* (placed on their sides).
6. **Second fermentation**   This starts in the bottle about six weeks after bottling.
7. **Remuage**   A methodical daily shaking, over a period of several months, on racks called *pupitres*. The bottles are placed at a slightly higher angle after each shake. The object is to dislodge the sediment (i.e. the dead yeast cells) until it collects on the cork with the bottle in an upside-down vertical position. The remuage takes place after three, four, or five years.
8. **Maturation**   This takes place in the upside-down position called 'sur le pointe'. This may be for one or several more years. It matures until required for shipping.
9. **Dégorgement**   The French name for the removal of the sediment which has collected on the cork. The bottle neck is frozen and the sediment is expertly ejected with the ice when the cork is removed.

*A* remueur *at work in a champagne cellar*

**10. Dosage** Champagne which was lost during dégorgement is replaced by more similar wine, and a sugar solution is added (known as *liqueûr de l'expédition*) if required in the final wine. After the *dosage* has been added the permanent cork is forced in and it is wired up and dressed in foil.

**11. Shipping** Champagne is regularly shipped to more than 160 nations.

### Sweetness in champagne

The sweetness in champagne is indicated on the label as follows:

*brut*  
*natur* } very dry (*I° Baume*)  
*for the English market*—  
a recent term which also means very dry  
*sec*—medium dry  
*demi-sec*—medium sweet  
*demi-doux*—sweet  
*rich*  
*doux* } very sweet (*7° Baume*)

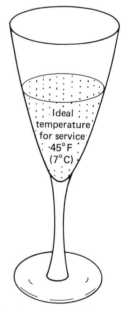

*A champagne flute*

16

Sweden and the USSR have traditionally preferred their champagne sweet, while the UK has favoured dry.

Champagne is often sold in bottles which are larger than those used for other wines. The *magnum*, which is the double-sized bottle, is used in several other regions (for example, Bordeaux). The *Jeroboam* (four bottles), the *Methuselah* (eight bottles), the *Salmanazar* (twelve bottles), the *Balthazar* (sixteen bottles) and the *Nebuchadnezzar* (twenty bottles) are sold less frequently for special celebrations and festivities.

Producers of sparkling wines in other regions of France and in many other countries use the méthode champenoise if optimum quality is their aim.

Sparkling wines are also made by three other methods:

## Cuve close

This method of making sparkling wine was started in France by M. Charmat, and involves secondary fermentation in large sealed tanks. This process of secondary fermentation takes only ten days to complete, in contrast to the years of patient waiting required by the *méthode champenoise*. The resulting wine is therefore very much cheaper than champagne.

## Transfer method

This is a similar method to the one used for making champagne, except that it is shortened by using *filtration* and *fining* instead of the lengthy remuage and maturation. *Kriter* is made in this way.

## Impregnation

This is the cheapest way of making sparkling wine. Carbon dioxide gas is put into the wine from a cylinder in much the same way as in the making of artificial mineral waters.

Whichever method is used will be directly related to the price the consumer will have to pay. The label on a bottle of champagne will not proclaim its method of manufacture as it is well known that champagne can only be made by the *méthode champenoise*. Other sparkling wines will state on the label the method used. If the sparkle was achieved by the tank system it will state 'Cuve Close' prominently on the label for the purchaser to see. New EEC legislation makes it illegal for wines which are made by the *méthode champenoise* outside Champagne to include 'méthode champenoise' on the label.

# Bordeaux

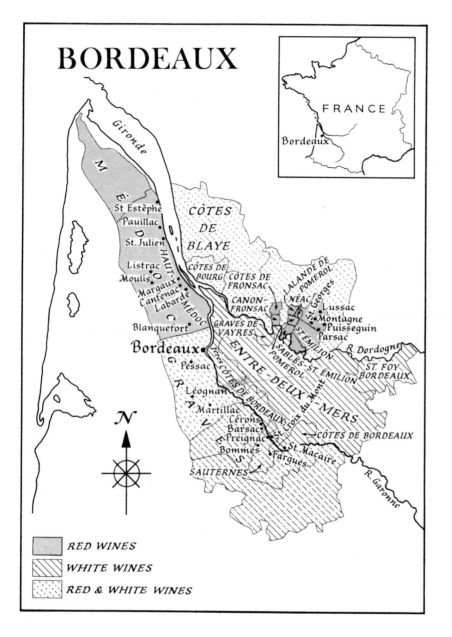

Bordeaux produces only about one-twentieth of the wine of France but its wines are of remarkable quality. One half of the *fine* wine of France is made in Bordeaux. The city has grown as a centre for wine exports since Roman times. Between 1154 and 1453 the area belonged to England following the marriage of *Eleanor of Aquitaine* to Henry, Duke of Dijon, who became *Henry II of England*. This French connection guaranteed a regular supply of wine for the English.

Chatham dockyard was built in AD 1200 so that a fleet of special ships could transport the wine to England and return to France with wool. The international unit of water displacement, known as 'Thames Tonnage', was invented to gauge the amount of cargo carried. The Dukes of Burgundy brought the trade to an abrupt end by defeating the English forces at the *battle of Castillon.* Many of the châteaux of Bordeaux have English names because of the historical association.

## Red wines of Bordeaux

There are six permitted black grape varieties which may be used in different proportions at each château. The *Cabernet Sauvignon* with its characteristic cedar-wood bouquet, gives *claret* its keeping quality and is predominant in *Médoc* wines. The *Merlot* is used more in *St-Emilion* and *Pomerol* wines, north of the *Dordogne* river, which are usually 1° higher in alcohol, and which mature earlier than Medocs. Red wines are also produced in the *Premières Côtes de Bordeaux, Bourg,* and a little in *Blaye.* The region of *Graves* also produces exceptional quality reds.

## White wines of Bordeaux

*Sauternes* and the areas of *Barsac* and *Cerons,* south of the river *Garonne,* and *Loupiac, Ste Croix du Mont,* and *Ste Macaire* north of the river, all produce superb sweet white wines made from grapes which have been allowed to develop a mouldy growth by being left on the vine long after the normal time of harvest. This condition is known as *Botrytis cinerea* (Latin) or 'noble rot'. The grapes are picked individually and each bunch may be visited as many as eight times. The shrivelled grapes contain very little juice.

Fine quality medium white wines are made in the *Graves* region and excellent dry whites in *Entre-deux-Mers* and *Blaye. Sauvignon* and *Semillon* are the main white grapes used in Bordeaux.

## The 1855 classification

The wines of the Gironde (Médoc, Graves and Sauternes), were put into groups according to their quality (prices over a period of years), in time for the Paris Exhibition of 1856. The first grouping of the Médoc was called 'Premièrs Grands Crus Classés' which means 'first great growths classified', and included *Château Latour, Château Margaux, Château Lafite-Rothschild,* and *Château Haut-Brion* (Graves). Second, third, fourth, and fifth groups followed in turn, each with a list of châteaux named. *Bourgeois* crus are the best of the remaining châteaux which were not included in the classification proper.

The only change which has taken place since 1855 was in *1973* when *Château Mouton-Rothschild* was moved up from 'deuxièmes' (second) to 'premièrs' (first) Grands Crus Classés.

# Burgundy

To begin to understand the wines of Burgundy one must appreciate the effects of the *French Revolution* in 1789, when the peasants marched from Marseilles to rid themselves of a self-indulgent and corrupt aristocracy. As they stormed up through the Rhône valley into Burgundy and

CHABLIS

CÔTE de NUITS

CÔTE de BEAUNE

CÔTE CHALONNAISE

CÔTE MÂCONNAISE

BEAUJOLAIS

on to Paris (where the seige of the city took two years), the revolutionary forces attacked church properties and large estates. Vineyards were divided up and many great properties became dozens of small *clos* (enclosures) or estates. Burgundy wines are not therefore known by château names.

Most small-scale wine-makers sell their wine to *négociants* who blend the wine and sell it to shippers. This has led to some suspicion about the changes which take place before the wine reaches the consumer. Most wines are sold under commune names but there are many individual wines known as Grand Cru, Premier Cru, etc. Burgundy is more than 400 miles from the nearest coast, which meant that the exporting of the wines had to be by bullock cart to the coast, adding to the number of people handling the wine.

Burgundy wines have been likened to the brass section of the orchestra while clarets take the place of the strings. They are mostly big and strong and of great body and bouquet.

The white wines of the *Côte de Beaune* are probably the finest dry white wines of the world. The *Chardonnay* is the variety of grape used for all north Burgundy white wines; this group includes Chablis, which is regarded as a Burgundy although it is nearly 100 kilometres away to the north-west. The northern red wines are made from the *Pinot Noir* grape.

The quality of Burgundy wines, if price is the deciding factor, decreases as you travel down Burgundy from north to south. The *Côte de Nuits* and the *Côte de Beaune* together are known as the *Côte d'Or* (slopes of gold). The *Hospices de Beaune* is a hospital charity run by nuns of the order of Little Sisters of Mercy. It is supported by visits from 200 000 tourists each year and the proceeds of a wine auction which is held on the third Sunday in November. The Hospice has its own vineyards, 130 acres bequeathed by thankful patients from the Burgundy region since the Hospice was founded by *Nicolas Rolin* in 1443. The prices at the auction are usually more expensive than in the towns, because the money is for charity work at the Hospice, but they serve as a guide to people's expectations of price increases.

*The Côte Chalonnaise* (region of Mercurey) produces all types of table wine, and from this point southwards begins the gradual change of vine varieties to the *Aligoté* (white) and *Gamay* (black). The *Mâconnais* produces very good red and white wines, the most famous being *Pouilly-Fuissé*.

*Vin de L'Année* (wine of the year) is produced in Beaujolais and often called Beaujolais *Primeur* or *Nouveau*. It is almost impossible to believe that more than one-third of the produce of Beaujolais is sold in one night to the English market. The third Thursday in *November* is the release date and many races are held to be the first in certain areas of the UK to serve the new wine, most of which will be drunk before Christmas (in the year of production). It is made by fermenting the wine from the *Gamay* juice which has been quickly separated from the tannin-bearing stalks. This means the wine will be less bitter and more palatable sooner. *Passe-tout-grains* is a wine blend of one-third Pinot Noir and two-thirds Gamay.

# The Rhône Valley

## Northern Rhône

The area is characterised by steeply terraced vineyards.

Main grape varieties—black Syrah and white Viognier.

*Côte Rôtie* (Literally meaning roasted slopes). Two miles of fine red wines.

*Condrieu* Dry white wines.

*Château Grillet* A vineyard of just over one hectare producing a much-prized dry white wine.

*Hermitage* Chapel on the hill built in the twelfth century by a soldier who returned from the Crusades. Three miles of vines producing red and white wines. *Crozes-Hermitage* are of slightly lower quality. Reds aged in wood for up to five years.

*St Joseph* Excellent red and white wines.

*Cornas* Fine quality red wine.

*St Peray* and *Clairette de Die* Sparkling wines, made by the méthode champenoise.

Between the Northern and Southern regions there is a stretch of 40 kilometres with few vines. (Most of the land is used for growing olives, apples, melons, etc.)

## Southern Rhône

On these gently sloping hillsides the main grape variety is the Grenache.

*Tavel* Best French dry rosé wine. Growers (170) work in co-operatives.

*Lirac* Red and rosé for export. White wine drunk locally only.

*Rasteau* Vin Doux Naturel. Lightly fortified white wine.

*Beaumes-de-venise* Sweet dessert wine from Muscat grape. Some VDN and also some red wine produced.

*Gigondas* Red, white and rosé wine. Minimum 12.5 per cent alcohol for red and rosé.

*Châteauneuf-du-Pape* 99 per cent red wine and 1 per cent white wine. There are thirteen *grape varieties* allowed in châteauneuf-du-pape. By law, the wine must always reach 12.5 per cent alcohol. There are 483 growers on 2020 hectares of vineyards.

*Lavender* and *thyme* have always been grown in these famous vineyards. The soil is stony, consisting of large cobbles called *pudding stones,* which retain moisture at night and reflect heat during the day.

The Baron Le Roy de Boiseaumarie founded the vineyard in the twelfth century, and his descendants instituted controls which became the model for the *Appellation Contrôlée* laws of all France.

Because of the blustery and sometimes violent *mistral* wind which blows down the valley from the north-west, wind-breaks of cypress, conifers and olive trees are found among the vines to protect them. *Samuel Pepys* and *Dr Johnson* spoke of Rhône wine as equal to claret. Could it be that perhaps these wines were better before Phylloxera? Rhône wines are generally higher in alcohol than other French wines.

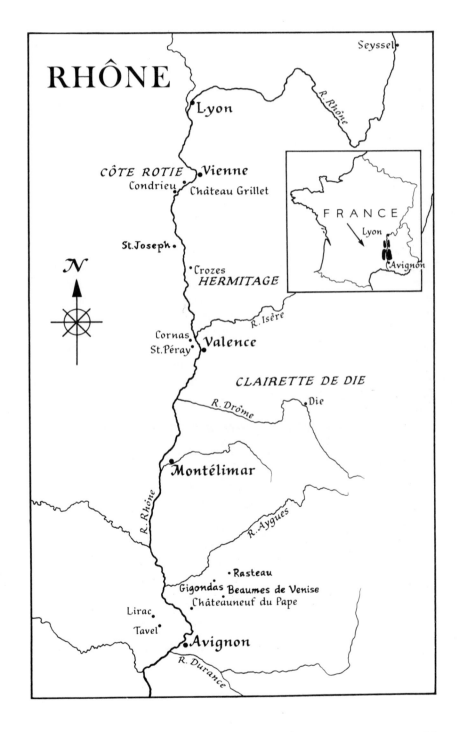

# Alsace

Alsace produces fine quality *dry white* wines. Other types of wine are rarely found in this part of France. The vines grow on eastern slopes of the *Vosges* mountains, in a narrow strip never wider than three kilometres and 115 kilometres long from north to south. Lower down the slopes the river *Ill*, from which Alsace derived its name, makes its cautious way northwards to pass through *Strasbourg*, spoken of as the crossroads of Europe, and then to join the mighty *river Rhine*.

Because of its position on the border between France and Germany, Alsace has always been disputed territory. The argument that the Vosges would make a better border than the river Rhine is still favoured by some folk. Both the languages are spoken as a result of the territory changing hands on so many occasions. The historical facts are: Alsace was *French* before 870(AD).

*German* from 870–1681.
*French* from 1681–1870.
*German* from 1870–1918.
*French* from 1918–1940.
*German* from 1940–1944.
*French* since 1945.

Viticulturally, the Alsatians have benefited from these changes as they seem to have combined together the best of both the German and French methods. The vine varieties grown in Alsace are names which we associate more familiarly with Germany.

All Alsace AOC wines must *by law* be bottled in Alsace. This prevents the possibility of fraud and contravention of the labelling regulations. The grape variety used in the wine is prominently displayed on the label as is the custom in Germany. The village or vineyard name is rarely shown on an Alsace wine label.

*A Dopff wine label*

Vines grow in Alsace to a height of *two metres*. This helps to give some protection from frost.

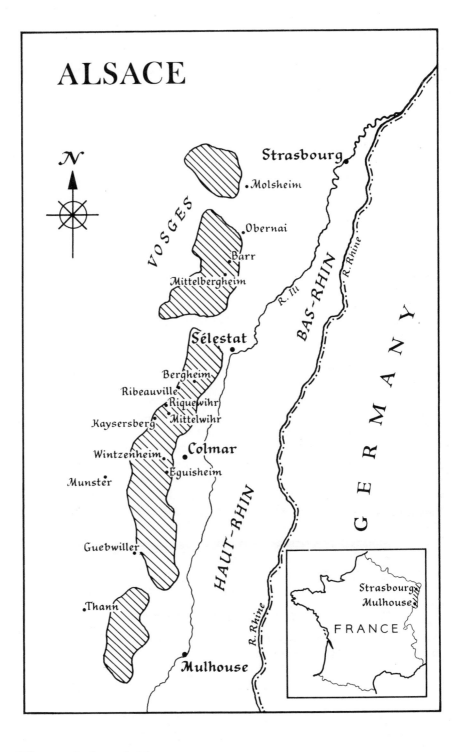

# ALSACE

Strasbourg
• Molsheim

VOSGES

• Obernai

• Barr

Mittelbergheim

R. Ill

BAS-RHIN

R. Rhine

Sélestat

Bergheim
Ribeauville •
• Riquewihr
Kaysersberg • • Mittelwihr
Wintzenheim • • Colmar
• Eguisheim
• Munster

GERMANY

HAUT-RHIN

Guebwiller •

R. Rhine

• Thann

Mulhouse

Strasbourg
Mulhouse

FRANCE

*Vine varieties of Alsace*

Chasselas
*Sylvaner
*Riesling
*Pinot blanc

*Muscat
*Gewurtzträminer
*Tokay Pinot gris

Vines marked with an asterisk are known as 'Noble' wines of Alsace. *Zwicker* is the term on the label which indicates that the contents of the bottle are made up of wines from a blend of grapes, including non-noble varieties. *Edelzwicker* describes wines which are made from a blend of grapes which are all of noble origin.

Sixty per cent of all the wine produced in Alsace is made from either the chasselas or the Sylvaner grape. The Tokay Pinot gris listed above should not be confused with the Hungarian wine Tokay, which is made from different grape varieties. The Traminer vine is often referred to as the *Gewürtz-traminer,* which is the German name for the same vine. Most Alsace wines should be drunk young—under eight years old.

# Loire

The distance from the Atlantic coast to Pouilly-sur-Loire is approximately 300 miles, during which the river Loire passes through some of the finest scenery in France. The 'Garden of France', as the valley is sometimes called, includes orchards, vineyards, fields of corn, and sugar-beet amongst its garden crops. The wines of the Loire valley are equally varied, more varied in fact than in any other French viticultural region.

The English connection with the area dates back to the twelfth century when Eleanor of Aquitaine, the thirty-year-old ex-wife of the King of France, married the youthful Duke of Dijon, who was only nineteen. By this marriage the Duke, who later became Henry II of England, gained control over the whole western seaboard of France, south of the river Loire. The marriage was a stormy one. Henry deserted Eleanor for a mistress and had his wife imprisoned; but Eleanor plotted successfully with their four sons to join the nobles, and together they finally forced their father to plead for peace. King Richard I (the Lion-heart) and King John were two of these four sons.

Princes and nobles built extravagant châteaux on the banks of the river, from where they could hunt the wild game of the densely-wooded area—the château of Saumur is an elegant example of the lifestyle of the local rulers of the time. The city of *Saumur* is world famous for its riding academy as well as its sparkling wine, made by the *méthode champenoise*. *Vouvray,* in the Touraine, also produces a fine quality sparkling wine made by this method.

The main tourist town of the Loire valley is *Tours*, a small and pretty town in Touraine, whose streets are thronged with tourists every summer.

*Anjou Rosé* is probably the best known wine of the whole valley, with a range of sweetness from medium-sweet to medium-dry. Its main centre of sale is *Angers*. Orléans is famous, not only for Joan of Arc who inspired the French to drive the English out of France, but also for its vinegar-makers.

The very fine dry white wines of the Loire, *Muscadet,* in the Pays Nantais, near the Atlantic coast, and *Sancerre, Pouilly-sur-Loire* and *Pouilly Blanc Fumé* in Central Loire, furthest from the sea, are all

A *Loire château*

superb and are particularly good accompaniments to sea-food, especially shell-fish. Care must be taken not to confuse the Pouilly wines of the Loire valley with the famous *Pouilly-Fuissé* of the Mâconnais in Burgundy.

The red wines of the Touraine, *Chinon, Bourgueil* and *St Nicolas de Bourgueil*, are fairly light in body and some customers may ask to have the *Chinon* lightly chilled. Sweet white wines are found in the Loire region near *Vouvray*, and at *Montlouis*, and a delightful sweet white wine made from over-ripe grapes at *Côteaux du Layon*.

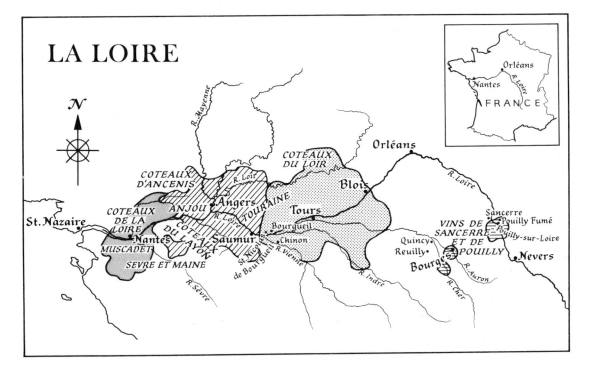

# The Midi and the South

The wines of the southern strip are largely undistinguished but very drinkable. They are produced mainly in co-operatives in vast quantities, accounting for more than one-half of France's total wine production. The most common grape varieties are the black Grenache grape and the white Carignan grape.

*The southern strip*

## Roussillon

*The Côtes du Roussillon* produces red, rosé and a little white wine. The *Côtes du Roussillon Villages* is a red wine area. Both are AC and provide the best red wines of the southern strip. The red wines need time to mature and will continue to improve for longer than most other southern reds; a shelf-life of twenty years is not unreasonable. Twenty-five communes are included in the appellation 'Côtes du Roussillon Villages'.

## Corbières

Corbières is the largest in area of all the VDQS appellations of the southern region. Red and rosé wines with a pronounced 'herby' flavour make up the bulk of production with a small amount of white wine.

*Fitou* is an AC wine of high quality from the south-east corner of Corbières. It is all red and has a minimum alcohol content of 12° OIML.

## Minervois

The wines from this area are lighter than those of Corbières and their quality varies enormously. Soft and fruity red and rosé wines are produced and also a little white. The wine carries the VDQS label and has a minimum of 11°OIML.

## Languedoc

An area with a great variety of wines; some of them are of excellent quality, such as St. Chinian, which is one of the VDQS local communes on the higher slopes. Most of the wines are light in character and nearly all are red or rosé.

## Costières du Gard

A VDQS area mainly producing red and rosé wines, which have a *maximum* alcohol content of 11°OIML. The area consists of a low group of hills south-east of Nîmes.

## Muscat de Frontignan

VDN (natural sweet wine, see page 84) produced near Sète from the partially fermented Muscat grapes, Grape spirit is added when the alcohol reaches 5°OIML. This takes the strength up to 15°OIML. The result is a sweet and fruity dessert wine.

### Provence

This area is noted for its fruity rosé wine with a minimum alcohol content of 11°OIML. Some red and white wines are also produced under the label 'AC Côtes de Provence'.

a) *Bandol* (AC). Tourist and fishing village east of Marseilles, famous for red wines aged in wood for a minimum eighteen months (unusual in south).

b) *Cassis* (AC). Produces the best white wine of Provence as well as some red and rosé. There is no connection with blackcurrants.

c) *Palette* (AC). Red, rosé and white wine from east of Aix-en-Provence. Château Simone, which produces a superb rosé, is the finest vineyard.

d) *Bellet* (AC). Red, white and rosé wine from north-west of Nice.

### Blanquette de Limoux

Thirty-four communes in the area round Limoux help to produce a white sparkling wine, made by the méthode champenoise.

### Vin de Pays

A large quantity of vins de pays is produced in the southern strip from the regions of Bouches-du-Rhône, Gard, Hérault, Aude, Pyrénées-Orientales, and Var. They are best described as typical wines of a particular region which satisfy certain standards laid down with regard to quality, yield per hectare, vine variety, etc.

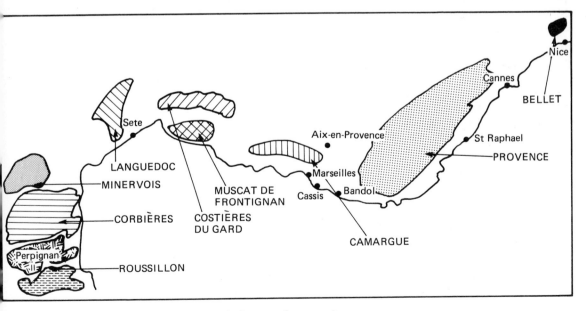

*Vineyards of the southern strip*

# Savoie

The region of Savoie is surrounded on all sides by the foothills of the Alps. The fresh, young, dry white wines of the area complement well the river and lake trout found here in abundance. Local white *truffles* are used to flavour the sauces which accompany the fine foods of Savoie.

The best known wine of Savoie is *Crépy*, made from the Chasselas vine. It is a dry white wine, sometimes *pétillant* (very slightly sparkling).

Sparkling *Seyssel*, sometimes made by the méthode champenoise, is an Appellation Controlée wine like its partner Crépy. The Rousette grape is used for Seyssel. This vine is used widely in Savoie, as shown on the map.

*Chambéry* is a fine quality French vermouth, made from both red and white local wine.

*Grenoble*, which is just south of Savoie, is the home of the liqueur *Chartreuse*, both green and yellow varieties. The secret recipe for this liqueur is known only to four *Carthusian* monks.

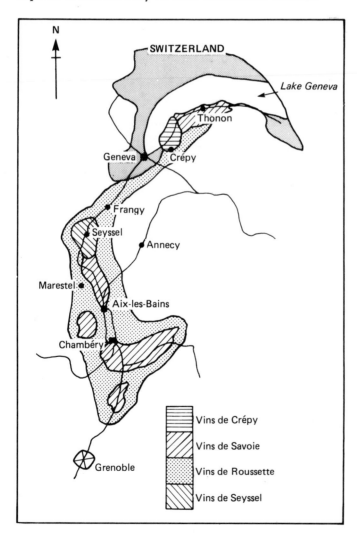

*The wine areas of Savoie*

# Jura

The most famous person from the Jura was *Louis Pasteur* who discovered that fermentation was the work of a living organism and not a chemical reaction. He lived and worked at *Arbois* (died 1895).

*Vin Fou* is the name given to the sparkling wine produced at Arbois (literally 'foolish wine') by Henri Maire.

*Château-Chalon* produces one of the most famous wines of France and certainly the longest keeping. Surprisingly, it is not a château but a small town. Its wine is known as *Vin Jaune* and is unique in France because of a yeast flor (scum), a crust which forms on the surface of the maturing wine. The wine is yellow or golden in colour and very dry and nutty in taste.

*Vin de Paille* (straw wine) is made from grapes which have been laid out on straw mats to dry. The resulting wine is very sweet and, like Vin Jaune, has a high alcoholic content.

*Vin Gris* is the name given to the delicately coloured rosé wine of the Jura.

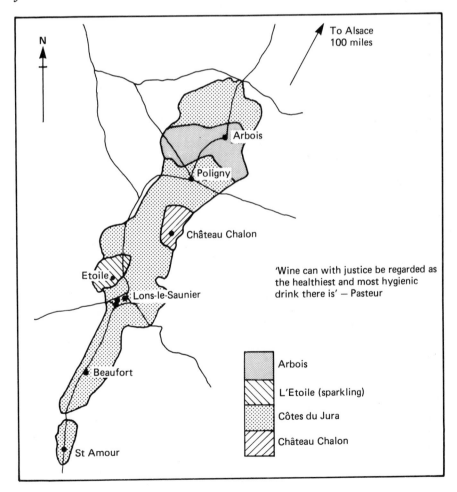

*The wine areas of the Jura*

# Germany

The largest proportion of German wine is white and low in alcohol. In the best years German white wines are equal to any wines in the world, but, due to its climatic position on the extreme limit of vine production, the number of great years is very small. Indeed almost half the vintages are of less than average quality. Because of the lack of variety of wines, and comparitively small production, Germany is of less importance to the wine consumer than some of its neighbours.

## Categories of wine

**Landwein**   Wine from a specific, named, local area.
**Tafelwein**   May be a blend of wines from EEC producers.
**Deutscher Tafelwein**   Made from German-grown grapes, minimum 8.5° OIML.
**Qualitätswein**   A blend of wine from a designated area.
**Qaulitätswein mit Prädikat**   Quality wine of distinction.
The *Prädikat* is the word which explains how the wine was made. For example:

*Kabinett*—special choice for grower's own sideboard.
*Spätlese*—wine from late-harvested grapes.
*Auslese*—wine from specially selected ripe parts of bunches of grapes.
*Beerenauslese*—wine from overripe fruit, grapes picked individually. Very expensive.
*Trockenbeerenauslese*—very sweet wine made from shrivelled grapes which have noble rot (*Edelfäule*). Very expensive.
*Eiswein*—wine made from grapes harvested while frozen. Beerenauslese sugar level.

*A German wine bottle and glass*

## Types of wine

**Hock**   German white Rhine wine.
**Steinwein**   Flinty dry wine of Franconia in dumpy Bocksbeutel bottles.
**Sekt**   Sparkling wine made in Germany.
**Deutscher Sekt**   German sparkling wine made with more than 60 per cent German-grown grapes.
**Spritzig**   Slight natural sparkle. (*Spritz* for short.)
**Red wine**   A small amount of light red wine is produced along the *Ahr* river and at the villages of *Bingen* and *Assmannshausen* in the region of Rheingau. *Baden* also produces some red and rosé wines.
**Liebfraumilch**   This blended Rhine wine was originally produced in the two-and-a-half hectares around the Liebfrauenstift monastery, at *Worms* in the Palatinate. It can now be made from blends of wines from any one of the four districts of Rheingau, Rheinhessen, Palatinate, or Nahe. (The name means 'the milk of the Church of Our Lady'.)

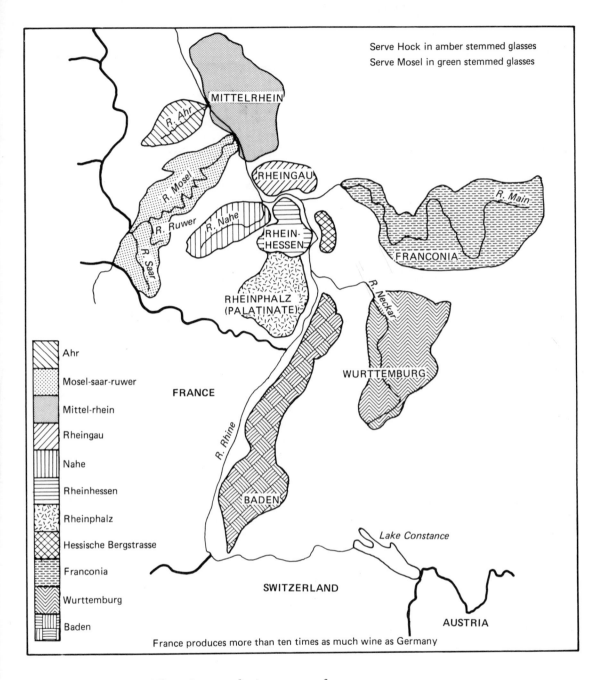

Serve Hock in amber stemmed glasses
Serve Mosel in green stemmed glasses

MITTELRHEIN

R. Ahr

R. Mosel

R. Ruwer

R. Saar

RHEINGAU

R. Nahe

RHEIN-
HESSEN

R. Main

FRANCONIA

RHEINPHALZ
(PALATINATE)

R. Neckar

WURTTEMBURG

FRANCE

R. Rhine

BADEN

Lake Constance

SWITZERLAND

AUSTRIA

France produces more than ten times as much wine as Germany

Legend:
- Ahr
- Mosel-saar-ruwer
- Mittel-rhein
- Rheingau
- Nahe
- Rheinhessen
- Rheinphalz
- Hessische Bergstrasse
- Franconia
- Wurttemburg
- Baden

*The wine-producing areas of Germany*

German wine labels usually show the grape variety used in the wine. *Müller-Thurgau* is the most widely used, but the *Riesling* (pronounced 'Reeceling') is regarded as the best quality vine. The *Sylvaner* for white wines and the *Spätburgunder* for red are also popular.

33

# Italy

*Garibaldi* founded modern Italy, now the greatest wine producing country in the world, by combining together into one nation a collection of native states. The wines of Italy are sometimes named after the variety of vine used, sometimes after the district, and in many cases after stories or legends. (For example, *Est! Est!! Est!!!* and *Lacryma Christi.*) Because of the abundant sunshine, Italian wines are normally higher in alcohol than most other European wines. Most Italian red wines also spend at least two years in wood.

Climatically, wines produced in the almost semi-tropical heel of the country are full, heavy and sweet, like *Locorotondo*; while in the far north of the country, in the foot hills of the Alps, and often in snowy conditions in the Alto-Adige, wines are produced in the Germanic style.

It is generally agreed that the finest red wines of Italy come from the northern half of the country and especially in the region of *Piedmont*. *Barolo* and *Barbaresco* are good examples. The southern half of Italy concentrates more on white wines. It is true to say that there is hardly a village in all Italy which does not produce wine.

## The Italian wine laws

The DOC laws presently in force were introduced largely as a result of the experience of the region of Tuscany, which introduced controls as long ago as 1932. Baron Ricasole at Castelli Brolio instituted the *black cockerel* symbol for the *Chianti Classico* wine. Classico means the centre, or heartland, of a region.

Italian law, unlike that of France, insists that it must be the local grower's organisation that applies for special labelling status and not the individual grower himself. The wine for which application is made must be a typical wine from the area (*vini typici*). It is equivalent to the French *vins de pays*.

*DOC (Denominazione di Origine Controllata)* corresponds roughly with *Appellation Contrôlée* of France, and *Qualitätswein* of Germany.

*DOCG (Denominazione di Origine Controllata et Garantita)* is the mark of exemplary distinction, awarded to only a few areas and controlled so strictly that, for instance, they are not allowed to be placed in containers of more than 5 litres. Examples of DOCG wines are *Barolo, Vina Nobile di Montepulciano,* and *Albana di Romagna*.

## Wines of particular interest

**Asti Spumante** (Piedmont)   A popular, sweet, white sparkling wine.
**Chianti** (Tuscany)   Red wine sold in raffia flasks known as *fiaschi.* Some top quality young chianti is made by the *Governo system*, whereby juice from semi-dried grapes is added to the wine in December, which leads to a new fermentation. It results in an added richness.
**Marsala** (Sicily)   Fortified wine originally produced by the Woodhouse brothers of England (for sale to Nelson's fleet). It can last for up to fifty years.
**Soave** (Veneto)   Dry white wine—delicate, light and sometimes slightly *pétillant*.

**Lambrusco** (Emilia-Romagna)   Frothy, *frizzante* (or *pétillant*) red and white wine. Can be on the sweet side and fruity.

**Frascati** (Latium)   Dry white wine made in the hills south of Rome.

**Lacryma Christi** (Campania)   'Tears of Christ', red and white, from Mount Vesuvius.

**Verdicchio** (Marches) Dry white wine from the east coast.

**Valpolicella** (Veneto)   A popular light red wine.

*Italian wine-producing areas*

# Spain

Spain is a very mountainous country, like an inverted soup-plate, with the central plateau around Madrid more than 668 metres above sea-level. The climate is very cold in winter and exceedingly hot in the high summer. There are more vines cultivated in Spain than in any other European country but the largest percentage are used for table grapes. The actual wine production is less than one-third of that of either Italy or France. Spanish wines are made from more than one hundred different vine varieties in as many styles as it is possible to imagine. Great improvements have been made in recent years to put Spain on a competitive footing with the fine wines of other European areas and scientifically-organised co-operatives are now being developed.

Approximately one-tenth of Spain's table wine is from *Rioja*, which is the finest wine-producing area in the country. The map of Rioja resembles a *bull* (see below). The river *Ebro* flows from the head to the tail, and the best quality wines are from around *Haro* near the head. The region is 75 miles long and produces fine red and white wines. When phylloxera devastated the vineyards of Bordeaux, the growers moved over the border and settled in Rioja. Vineyard names in Rioja are used as *brand names* for blends of local wines from near the property.

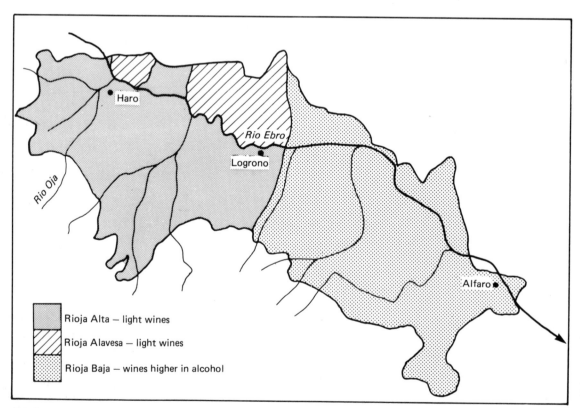

*Rioja*

SPAIN

*La Mancha,* the large region south of Madrid, produces vast quantities of wine, amounting to nearly half the total made in all Spain. Red, white, and rosé wines are made around Valdepenas, the main town.

*Alella* is a fairly good wine from Catalonia. It is not usually exported.

*Tarragona* is a red dessert wine from Catalonia.

*Malaga,* a fortified sweet white wine which has boiled grape juice added, was known in Victorian times as 'Mountain' (because of the hills behind Malaga).

*Muscatel* is a sweet white fortified wine from coastal districts.

*Galicia,* in north-west Spain, is well known for its 'green' wines similar to the Vinhos Verde of neigbouring Portugal. They have a slight natural sparkle.

Spain's best *sparkling wines* are made by the *méthode champenoise* at *San Sadurni de Noya* in the Penedes area of Catalonia, which has the largest concentration of sparkling wine production in the world. Perelada, a small wine-growing district in the same area, also makes sparkling wine but by the tank method of secondary fermentation.

The *Consejos Reguladores* control the *Denominación de Origen* (DO) in Spain.

## Terms used

*Tinto*—red *Vino de Mesa*—table wine *Seco*—dry.
*Rosado*—rosé *Consecha*—vintage (year) *Dulce*—sweet
*Blanco*—white *Vendimia*—vintage *Espumoso*—sparkling
*Sangria*—red wine containing citrus juice
 *4° Año*—bottled in fourth year after the harvest
Some Spanish table wines are fermented and matured in large earthen-
ware jars, 3 metres tall, called *tinajars*. The most famous wine made in
this way is *montilla*, the wine which is often mistakenly confused with
sherry. Tinajars are also used in La Mancha. •

*Tinajars*

# Portugal

Portugal is Britain's oldest ally—the two countries have been friendly
for over 1200 years. The friendship was improved by the *Treaty of
Windsor* in 1353 and in 1703 Portuguese wines received special benefits
from the *Methuen Treaty,* which gave them preferential advantages over
the wines of France. The financial advantage was that Portuguese wines
could enter Britain at a rate of import duty one-third less than that paid
by the French. The treaty does not apply to present trading but the
friendship continues.

Geographically, the north of Portugal is mountainous, while the
south beyond the river Tagus is flat. The better wines are found in the
rugged north in the hills, which are humid and wet except for the four
months of hot summer. The southern districts are nearly always dry and
sunny.

## The main wine-making districts

*Minho District* (in the north-west of Portugal) south of river Minho.
*Vinho verde* literally means 'green wine' but the word green refers to
the maturity of the grapes, and not the colour of the wine, and therefore
means young, fresh, immature, even underripe. Vinhos verdes can be
red, white, or rosé in colour. The vines in the Minho district are grown
high, often as high as six metres and trained over trees or trellises. The
wines produced are low in alcohol, dry in character, and have a delicate
refreshing natural sparkle.
*Douro region* (in the mountainous upper river Douro area). Because of
the steepness of the slate hillsides, the vineyards are built into terraces.
The Douro is most famous for port wine, but almost 70 per cent of the
wine produced is table wine (unfortified). The main centres of population in the mountains are the villages of Regua and Vila Real, where the
popular *mateus rosé* has long been established.
*Bairrada* (near the west coast, north of the Mondego river) is most
famous for its sparkling wines. The main town is *Agueda* and the region
is not so hilly as the other vine-growing areas of northern Portugal. Red
and white table wines are produced, as well as some rosé and some
sparkling wine made by the méthode champenoise.

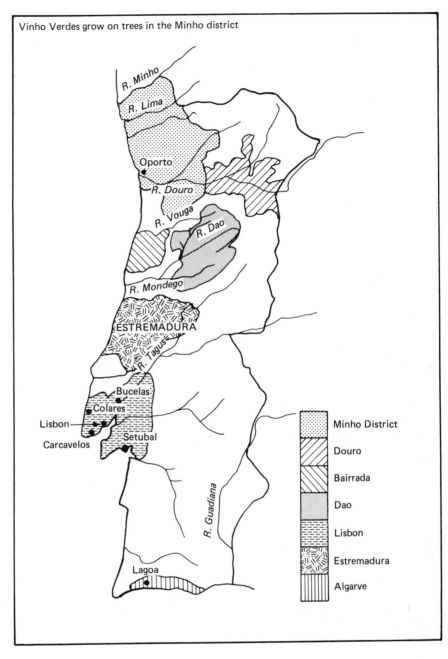

Vinho Verdes grow on trees in the Minho district

R. Minho
R. Lima
Oporto
R. Douro
R. Vouga
R. Dao
R. Mondego
ESTREMADURA
R. Tagus
Bucelas
Colares
Lisbon
Setubal
Carcavelos
R. Guadiana
Lagoa

Minho District
Douro
Bairrada
Dao
Lisbon
Estremadura
Algarve

*The wine-producing areas of*
*Portugal*

*Dão* (situated between the Dão and Modego rivers). The main town is *Viseu* and the wines produced are excellent reds and whites from co-operatives. *Grão Vasco* is probably the best-known wine of the region, while *terras altas* is sold widely in the United Kingdom. Most of the fermentation is done by modern auto-vinification methods and the wine is matured in large concrete *balloons* before blending. The reds are then blended and spend up to three further years in cask before sale.

39

*Lisbon* (capital of Portugal, main tourist centre). Hotels are fast replacing the vineyards around Lisbon.

*Colares*—red wine from the sandhills beyond the beach. The wines of Colares never suffered from the phylloxera outbreak.

*Carcavelos* produces dessert and sacramental wines.

*Setúbal* produces substantial sweet white Muscatel wines.

*Bucelas* is well known for its quality dry white wine.

*Lagoa* and *Estremadura* also produce good red and white table wines.

# Cyprus—Island of Wine

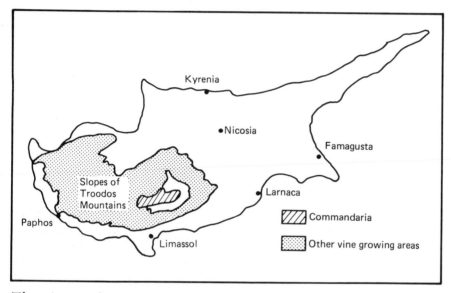

*The wine-producing areas of Cyprus*

Cyprus wines are amongst the earliest recorded in the world. More than *one-fifth* of the island's population is employed in the industries associated with grapes. The *climate* is such that the growers do not have to contend with the uncertainties which their Continental counterparts experience. Black grapes account for 85 per cent of the grapes grown on the island.

The types of wines produced in Cyprus are varied, the best known being the oldest known named wine in the world—*Commandaria St John*. Wines labelled *Cyprus sherry* have been produced for many years and have established an excellent reputation. Much in their production is similar to the Spanish tradition, for instance, *solera systems* are used in the warehouses for blending the final wine. Fino-style sherries are produced using a *cultivated flor*. Cream sherries are sweetened with old Commandaria, instead of the Spanish Pedro X which is not grown on the island. *Aphrodite* white wines are made from the local white grape 'Xinisteri'. Cyprus wines have never yet suffered an attack of *phylloxera*. Almost all the vines are *grafted* onto American root-stock to prevent the possibility of an outbreak.

40

All the wines, with the exception of Commandaria, are refrigerated to prevent a deposit of *tartrates* later. These crystals sometimes appear in wine when there is a sudden change of temperature. They are quite harmless, and may indeed be of benefit to health, but they are unacceptable to most people. Refrigeration enables the shipper to filter the crystals out before the wine is bottled, thus ensuring that they will not appear again.

## Commandaria St John

*St John's shield*

This *sweet red dessert wine* has a longer history of production than any other known wine. Records show that it dates back to the twelfth century, to the time of the Crusades. Sir Walter Raleigh was granted the monopoly of Commandaria St John by Queen Elizabeth I for services to the crown. Several varieties of grapes, blended together, are used in the making of Commandaria St John. Nearly 90 per cent are black grapes and the remaining 10 per cent are white. After the harvest the grapes are left on white corrugated paper mats, on the flat roof-tops, for fifteen days to reduce the water content. This wine is rich in *tannin*, ensuring that it will keep for many years. Fermentation is rapid, due to the hot climate, and cold water is thrown over the vats of fermenting must to slow down the rate of conversion from juice to wine and to give a better quality end-product.

The new Commandaria wine is added to old Commandaria wine in large casks from which wine is continually being taken. This means that the new wine will blend with the old wine in the same way as the Solera system in the sherry district of Jerez in Spain. A small bag of herbs is also suspended in the wine while it matures. The strength of Commandaria St John after a slight fortification with grape-spirit (brandy) is 27° Sikes (16° OIML).

## Fred Rossi

A serious study of the wines of Cyprus was undertaken in 1956 by Fred Rossi, with the objective of improving the island's wines. Over a seven-year study he matched many different vines, some which were already grown on the island and some which were not, with the soils from the different vine-bearing slopes. *The Rossi report* produced its first positive results just before Fred Rossi's death in 1964 and it has played a large part in the continuing improvement of the wines of Cyprus since that time.

## Geography and history

Whilst the vines are found all over the island of Cyprus, the greatest concentration and perhaps the best quality vines are on the slopes of the *Troodos* mountains.

Nearly all the Cyprus wines are pasteurised before export. This stabilises the wine and prevents secondary fermentation taking place in the bottle, which also removes the possibility of 'fizz' in the wine.

The British connection with the island began in 1878, when it was

41

ceded to the British government by the Turks. In 1960, after a bitter stuggle for independence, Cyprus became a republic. In 1974 the Turkish army invaded the northern part of the country and partitioned about one-third of the island for Turkey, leaving the mainly Greek population in the south.

The capital of Cyprus is Nicosia (in the north) but the wine trade and, more especially for the tourists, the wine festivals, are held in Paphos and Limassol, both in the south.

# South Africa

The colony's founder Jan Van Riebeeck planted the first vines in 1652. He was the surgeon on board the Dutch ship which made the first landing. Recorded in his diary of 2 February 1659 is the following:

> Today—God be praised—Wine pressed for the first time from Cape grapes, and from the virgin must, fresh from the co-op, a sample taken.

Governor Simon van der Stel, Van Riebeeck's successor, further developed the South African wine industry from Groot Constantia, near Cape Town.

The Cape wine growers received a boost which was very welcome when large numbers of Protestant Huguenots arrived from France. They had been forced to leave France hurriedly because of religious persecution. This was in 1688 and they were described at the time as landing on South African soil with the Bible in one hand and vines in the other. Many of them certainly had the necessary expertise to help, advise, and develop their own vineyards around the cape regions.

## KWV

The KWV (the South African wine-farmers' association) was founded in 1918 and is responsible now for more than 90 per cent of all the wine production in South Africa. Large co-operative wineries have been developed and the KWV assists the growers in advising on production techniques and the marketing of the wine. They are encouraging the vineyard owners to plant more French grape varieties, especially the Chenin Blanc white vine from the Loire, known as *steen* in South Africa, which is well suited to the soil and climate of the Cape. The black grape varieties, Pinot noir, Gamay, and Malbec are also increasing.

Farmers are persuaded to conform to KWV suggestions and failure to do so may result in restrictions being placed on individual growers, preventing them from selling any wine outside a radius of three miles from their vineyard entrance. Any surplus wine which growers may have is taken by the KWV and the association takes on the responsibility for its sale.

The vintage takes place in *April* or *May* and the physical work in the vineyards is done mainly by local black workers—so labour costs are fairly low. There is an abundant supply of land for cultivation, and if the world demand for Cape wines increases there is ample room for expansion in all areas. All the new vines planted in South Africa are grafted onto American root-stock to prevent phylloxera.

Fine quality sparkling wines are produced by the *cuve close* tank method of secondary fermentation. Liqueurs are also made, the most famous being Van Der Hum (meaning 'What's his name') from small tangerines.

The *Little Karoo* (little desert) region produces well-known South African sherry and port-type wines. The average rainfall here is not more than ten inches a year and the vineyards have to be irrigated. *Worcester, Robertson, Montagu,* and *Ladysmith* are all important centres. A natural 'flor' yeast growth first appeared on some casks of sherry in South Africa in 1933, thus enabling the wine-makers to produce *fino* sherries of a similar character to those from Andalucia in Spain. Soleras are used for the blending of South African sherry and the *Palomino* grape is the one most widely used.

The port-style wines which are made are of very high quality, the best being those produced by the KWV co-operatives, and good quality brandy is also distilled in South Africa.

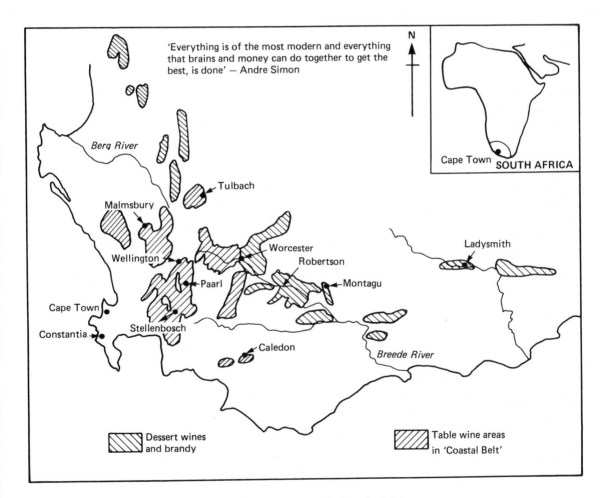

*The wine-producing areas of South Africa*

# Australia

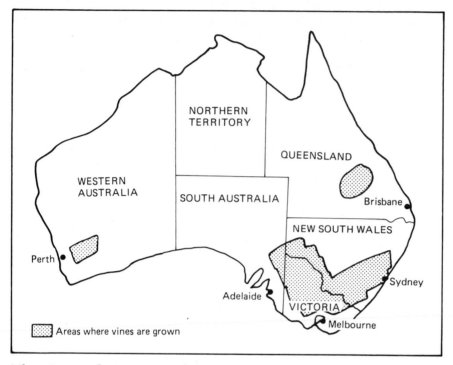

*The wine-producing areas of Australia*

In 1788 Governor *Arthur Phillip* planted the first vines, not very success-fully. In 1791 three acres were planted at *Parramatta* with the help of French prisoners of war sent from England. In 1820 *John MacArthur* planted the first commercial vineyards of Australia. His quarrel with *Captain Bligh* (of the 'Bounty'), who was Governor of New South Wales, led to his exile to Europe to study viticulture. *James Busby* was a teacher in an orphanage in the 1830s. His salary was set at £100, plus one-third of any sales made from the school garden. With the help of the boys, he planted a very successful vineyard and made a considerable amount of money from wine sales. But an excuse was found to remove him from his position, so he left Australia and came to Europe to attend courses in Montpellier. His contribution to the wine industry on his return to Australia was immeasurable.

In 1851 many thousands of Europeans went over to join the great Australian *gold rush*. They staked out their small parcels of land and dug furiously. A few were very successful, the largest find being a gold-bearing nugget from New South Wales, in 1872, which yielded 187 pounds of gold. The government came to the rescue of some of the unlucky prospectors by providing them with vine plants to raise on their small holdings. This venture was at *Rutherglen,* which produces sherry and port-type wines in the main.

The climate of Australia is, from a wine-maker's point of view, predictable. Seventy per cent of the vineyards have to be irrigated and a pure culture of yeast is used for the fermentation of the wine, instead of relying on the 'bloom' on the grapes. Because there is no uncertainty about the weather, the wines have a reliable standard of quality and vintages are unimportant. Many of the wines are known by their 'generic' European names—hock, claret, burgundy, etc.

The vintage takes place in Australia in March and April, and the method of viticulture and vinification are among the most modern in the world. As there is an abundance of land, the vines in most areas are planted wide apart, wide enough for vehicles to drive between the rows, which is an extravagance not possible in most European regions. In most cases the wines are produced in co-operatives, and 75 per cent of the wines of Australia are sold by way of *Adelaide* because of its proximity to the Murray and Barossa Valley regions.

Australian wines have declined in the UK in recent years, largely due to the end of *Imperial Preference* in 1976, after Britain joined the *EEC*, but also because of the decline which occurred in the Second World War when there was danger to shipping. Between 1939 and 1970, UK imports of Australian wine fell from three-and-a-half million gallons to less than one million.

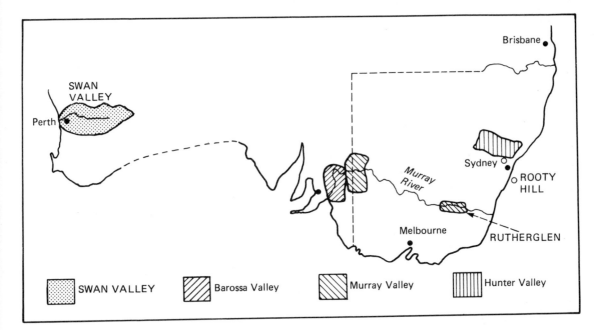

*Australian co-operative wineries*

45

# United States of America

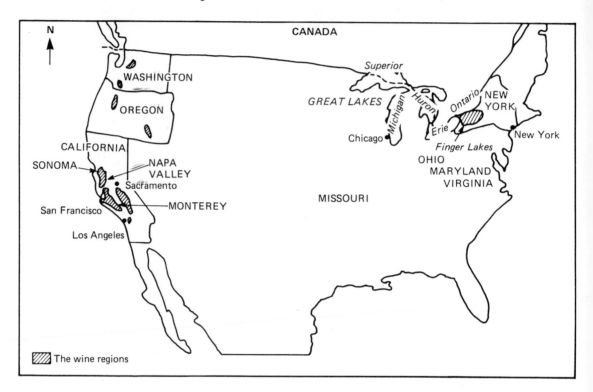

*The wine-producing areas of the USA*

## Finger Lakes

The climate of the Finger Lakes region of New York State in the east of the USA is similar to that of Germany, with hard cold winters and a short hot summer season. Lake Ontario and the long thin Finger Lakes contribute a tempering influence. The species of vine used is different from the European vine. The most common species planted is *Vitis Riparia* which, along with *Vitis Rupestris,* was found to be immune to phylloxera. Root-stocks from the Finger Lakes region are therefore used in Europe to prevent another outbreak of the problem, except in England, where most vines are grown on ungrafted roots. Since the 1950s some growers in New York State have been trying to establish the European vines in the Finger Lakes region because they consider *Vinifera* grapes to be of a higher standard.

    *Lesser known vineyards of the USA* are found in the states of Missouri, Ohio, Maryland, and Virginia, with substantial plantings being made in Oregon and also in Washington State.

## California

Vines were introduced to California by the Spanish Franciscan Mission Fathers for sacramental purposes.

The Californian climate is similar to that of the Mediterranean, with temperatures ranging from cool, similar to northern France, to very hot, like southern Italy or north Africa. Methods of vinification are among the most modern available. Wineries are very large, like ranches, with wide aisles between vine rows to enable the modern grape-picking machines to work along them.

## Varietal wines

These are the wines of North America, which are labelled after the main grape variety in the bottle. The best known examples are:

Zinfandel ⎫
Grenache ⎬ red
Cabernet ⎭

Sultana ⎫
Sauvignon vert ⎬ white
Chardonnay ⎭

The top quality varietal wines of California are known also as *premium wines* which can be compared with the French AOC wines. Fifty-one per cent must be of the grape variety named on the label.

## Generic wines

Generic wines are those which are named after the long established European areas. Many North American and Australian wines are labelled as claret, burgundy, chablis, sauternes, graves, hock, and even champagne. A substantial amount of Californian champagne is produced, but it would not be allowed into the UK under that name. A generic wine should possess the distinctive colour, flavour, and aroma of its European original.

## Napa Valley

This area is probably the finest red wine district in the USA. Count Haraszthy introduced the *Zinfandel* vine from his native Hungary in 1857. The classic *Cabernet Sauvignon*, known simply as *Cabernet* by the Americans, and the *Grenache* provide outstanding wines for the discerning Californian gourmets in one of the world's famous tourist areas. Fine white wine is also made. *Christian Brothers* are large producers.

## Sonoma Valley

The strong Italian connection has led to this northern Californian wine region being largely planted with Italian vines. *Buena Vista* is Count Haraszthy's original vineyard producing excellent wines. *Salinas* is a wine-producing region in South California, in the hotter area. *Paul Masson* and the *Wente Brothers* are two of the largest wine producers in the area between the forests of *Monterey* and *San Benito*.

# Hungary

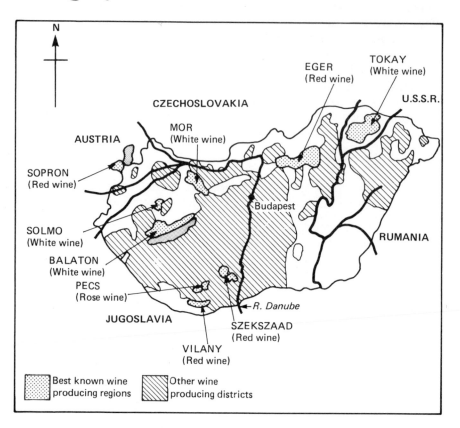

Hungarian wine-producing areas

Hungary is said to have been invaded more times than any other state in the world. Its wine industry is at present controlled by *Monimpex*, which is the state monopoly. No vineyard is privately owned. Some examples of the wines of Hungary which can be bought outside the country are:

*Bull's Blood*, the origins of which are steeped in history. In 1552 the Turks were beseiging the city of Eger. The Magyars fought so fiercely that the enemy decided that they must be drinking the blood of bulls. In fact it was the strong red wine of the area which kept the defenders strong! This wine improves with keeping.

*Olasz Riesling* is the white Italian riesling grape. It is grown in Hungary extensively and provides most of the everyday 'vin ordinaire'. Large plantings of this grape are found on the great plain of the river Danube and also north of Lake Balaton, where Hungarians spend their summer holidays on the golden sands beside the largest lake in Europe.

*Pecs Rosé* is a particularly fine dry rosé wine from the south of Hungary.

## Tokay

*Tokay Aszu* is made from Furmint and Harslevelu grapes which have been affected by *noble rot*. The sugar in the grapes has concentrated due to the effects of *botrytis cinerea,* the fungus which attacks the grapes that have been left on the vine for up to twelve weeks after the main harvest. Slow fermentation follows the individual picking of the over-ripe grapes.

Some of the best quality noble rot grapes are selected for special crushing to form the pulp for *puttonyok*. This is a seven-gallon container of grape-flesh which may be added to the one-year old wine. The quality and degree of sweetness of Tokay Aszu is indicated on the neck label which states how many 'Putts' or 'Puttonyos' have been added. The figure may be 3, 4, or 5 puttonyos. The German wine Beerenauslese would be equal to 5 Putts if comparisons were possible.

An old Hungarian saying that, 'Everyone bows to Tokay', is a comment on the country's turbulent history, when caves were dug in the hillsides surrounding the vineyards to protect the wine from invaders. As the caves were, and in many cases still are, less than 1.3 metres in height, it was necessary to bow the head to enter.

After storage for six or seven years in 35-gallon oak barrels, called *gonci*, the sweet wine will satisfy the gourmet either as an accompaniment to a fine quality dessert or as a drink on its own.

The word *Szamorodni* literally means 'as it comes' and indicates that the Tokay has been made in the normal way without the use of any noble rot grapes. Szamorodni Tokay may be either sweet or dry.

*Note* Tokay wine is bottled in 50 cl bottles.

*A Hungarian wine label*

# Vineyards of England and Wales

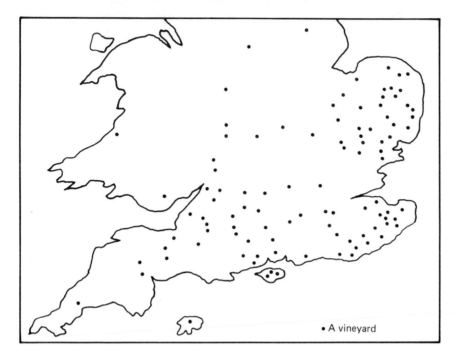

*English vineyards*

The revival of wine-making in England was pioneered by Guy Salisbury-Jones at Hambledon in Hampshire in 1951. The latitude of the British Isles, at the extreme climatic limit of the wine-grower's world, makes such a commercial enterprise a precarious one. The debits include winds, frost, rain (all at the most unwelcome times!), mildew, insects (especially wasps), starlings, hares, and the Customs and Excise Office, to name but a few! On the credit side is the ingenuity and devotion of the wine grower. Only in rare years does the record of sunny days reach the *one hundred days* between the flowering and the vintage, which on the continent of Europe is regarded as necessary to produce good wines. The 120 days required for a great wine would be a blessing indeed!

In 1066, at the time of the Norman Conquest, the French invaders found vineyards which had been established by the Roman legions. Although the British were largely drinkers of beer, the thirst for wine had remained strong. The French improved our agricultural methods and whetted our appetites for claret. The vineyards of England prospered until the sixteenth century when they were nationalised by King Henry VIII at the time of the dissolution of the monasteries. As most of the vineyards were either church-owned, or of royal estate, the decline was swift.

The UK climate is maritime and it is probably more akin to Bordeaux than the Rhine. So, although decent English white wine is now produced, experiments are continuing at many English vineyards, notably at *Three Choirs* in Gloucestershire, and at *Westbury* in Berkshire, where the first fine quality English red wine has been produced. The experiments to determine which variety of vine stock best suits our native soil and climate will benefit all the wine-growers and drinkers of home-produced wines, and the English Vineyards Association has been formed to enable growers to share their expertise. English wines have recently been awarded merits at Continental wine festivals.

# Other Wine-producing Countries

**USSR.** Although reliable statistics are not available, it is thought that Russia produces about 700 million gallons of wine each year. The best Russian wines are from vines grown on the limestone slopes near *Yalta* in the *Crimea*. A wine similar to champagne is also made there. In *Moldavia* very good brandy and sparkling wines are made. *Georgia* produces excellent red wine, rich in iron. *White Russia* is almost too far north but produces dry white wines. However, very few wines from the USSR find their way to the UK.

*The main wine-producing areas of the USSR*

**Austria.** The Austrian wine industry suffered a severe set-back in 1985 with the discovery of the chemical *diethylene glycol* in wines offered for sale in England. Scandals of this nature take years to overcome.

A sweet white wine called *Gumpoldskirchener* is Austria's best-loved wine. *Schluck* and *Blue Danube* are popular medium-dry wines sold in the UK.

**Switzerland** produces good wines in three main districts. (1) *Vaud*: its dry white wine called *Le Chablais* should not be confused with the chablis of Burgundy. (2) *Valais*: dry white *Fendant* and excellent red *Dole* are very popular, as are the famous *glacier wines* which are carried up the mountains to mature in caves above the snow line. (3) *Lake Neuchâtel* (means 'new castle'): makes dry white wine with a slight natural sparkle.

**Yugoslavia** is reputed to be where Noah planted his vines (see Genesis 9.20–21 for the first printed record of drunkenness). *Lutomer* wines are among the most popular in Britain (in particular, *Laski Riesling*). They are in the low-price bracket and of medium taste. *Tiger Milk* is a medium-sweet wine. The Yugoslav wine industry is operated by a State monopoly.

**Bulgaria, Czechoslovakia, and Rumania** also have their wine industries controlled by the State. Large amounts are produced but very little reaches Britain, except for the popular Bulgarian Cabernet Sauvignon.

**Turkey** is a small producer of undistinguished wines. The vast vineyard areas grow grapes for use as raisins, sultanas, currants, and as dessert grapes.

**Greece** also produces grapes for wine and dried fruit. Two wines are worthy of mention, *Retsina*, with its unusual pine-forest flavour of resin, and *Mavrodaphne*, a rich, sweet dessert wine. Both taste best with Greek food on a Greek island.

**Israel**. Since the injection of capital and technical help from Baron Philippe de Rothschilde the winemakers have reached a very high level of wine, with vineyards irrigated by sprinklers with water from the river Jordan.

**Algeria, Tunisia, and Morocco** are all small wine-producing countries.

**Lebanon** is famous for *Château Musar*, a good red wine from Bekaá valley.

**Kashmir**, in the Himalayas, has produced wine for over 400 years.

**South America.** Argentina is the largest producer, Mendoza and San Juan being well known regions. Chile produces the finest wine. Brazil, Uruguay, Paraguay, and Bolivia all produce wine for home use.

**Canada** produces good wines by modern methods near Ontario.

**New Zealand** produces small quantities of high quality wine, some of which is obtainable in the UK. Prominent among them are *Cook's Chenin Blanc* and *Montana Cabernet Sauvignon*.

# Part 3:
# The Service of Wine

*Serving of Wine*
*Sparkling Wine*
*Tasting Techniques*
*Glassware*
*Handling Glassware*
*Temperatures for Wine*
*Labelling*
*Decanting*

# Serving Wine

In the following sequence of photographs the service of wine is demonstrated by Julie and Sandy. A white Californian wine and a claret are being served to a party of three guests.

1. Julie takes the order on the right of the host. This is the 'point of sale' and a smile is guaranteed to increase turnover.

2. The wine is presented to the host on a clean napkin so that he can verify his choice before the cork is removed.

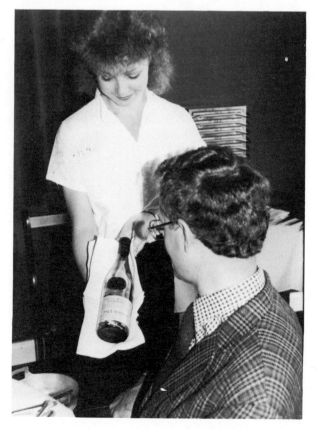

3. A small amount of the foil or plastic capsule should be removed. Sandy is seen cutting the capsule just below the top of the bottle.

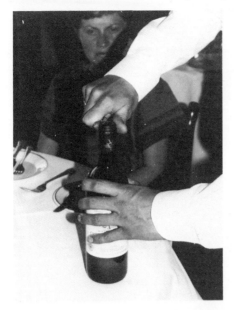

4. The white wine has been placed near to the right of the host in a wine-cooler filled to the shoulder of the bottle with ice and water. The cooler has been dressed with a clean white napkin, which may later be used by the host to dry the bottle if the waiter is too busy to return to top up the glasses. The waiter may use this napkin when serving the wine. The handles of the ice-bucket have been used to hold the napkin in place. If there were no handles, the napkin could have been hung neatly over the side of the stand, or carefully placed over the bottle in a narrow fold.

5. The capsule of the Paul Masson white wine is being cut by Julie. The small piece may be placed in a pocket or dropped into the cooler.

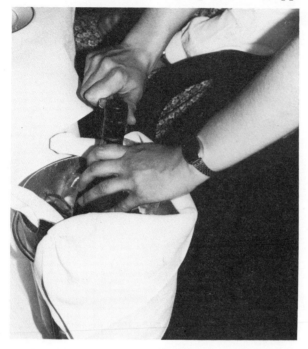

6. The top of the cork should be wiped at this stage to remove any mould or dirt which may spoil the wine. Julie is using the napkin which was around the cooler. She will replace it before finally leaving the table.

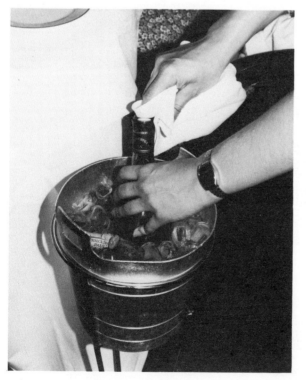

7. Julie is removing the cork from the white wine. Notice that she is doing so with the wine still in the cooler. The knuckle of one hand is held against the angle of the 'waiter's friend' so that it will not slip off the edge of the bottle top. The other hand is used to lever the cork out by lifting the long arm of the extractor. Care should be taken when screwing down into the cork that the screw does not go down on an angle, as this is almost certain to cause the cork to break if the corkscrew reaches the side of the bottle.

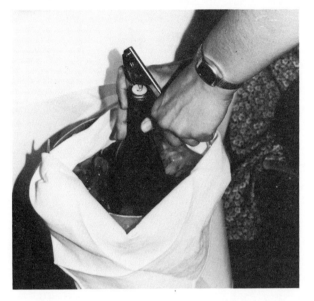

8. Sandy has completed the removal of the cork from the Château Charron red wine. He will smell the cork and place it in his pocket. He will then wipe the bottle top once again with the napkin.

9. He pours a little wine into the host's glass for him to taste. When pouring the wine, from the host's right, and at all times during the service, the label should be clearly visible. A folded napkin should be held by the waiter while pouring. This is used to wipe the top of the bottle after each pour.

10. Julie pours the white wine for the host. He can read the label as she pours. Her right index finger is placed vertically over the shoulder of the bottle. As she finishes pouring she will gently twist the bottle neck to avoid any drips, but the napkin is held folded in the left-hand just in case. *Note:* It is not easy to display the bottle label to the customer if you pour with the left-hand.

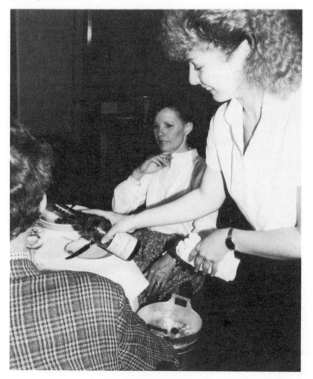

11. Julie waits while the host tastes the wine. If he approves the wine she will move to the lady on his right and fill her glass to between one-half and two-thirds full. It is usual to move to the right around the table serving any ladies present first, continuing around the table and serving the gentlemen, leaving the host until the last, when his glass is filled to the same level.

12. Sandy has just completed serving the second lady, and is wiping the bottle top before going on to top up the host's glass. He will then place the claret on a napkin on a side-plate, on the table, and not too far from the host's right hand, with the label facing the host. The cork may also be left on this side-plate. The good sommelier will anticipate and return to top up the glasses when required, and will enquire at the opportune moment if another bottle is needed.

# Sparkling Wine

## Opening

Champagne and sparkling wine should be served at a temperature of between 7°C and 8°C (45°F to 47°F), reached by placing the bottle in an ice-bucket with ice and water for thirty minutes or so, or in a refrigerator for about one-and-a-half hours. Sparkling wine which is well chilled will effervesce much less than if it is opened unchilled.

## Serving

The bottle of wine should be lifted from the ice-bucket and quickly dried with a clean table-napkin. It should be presented to the host on his right-hand side so that he can check the label.

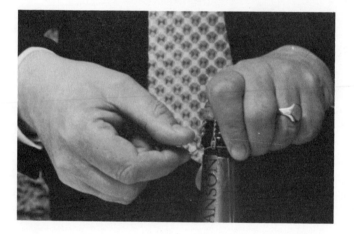

The retaining muzzle wire must be loosened so that the cork can be released. The foil should be cut just below the wire and not torn roughly away. This leaves a presentable appearance. The foil from around the wire should be removed.

Place the bottle on a flat table surface and, with one thumb covering the top of the cork, untwist the retaining wire until it is loose.

The muzzle and its dressing should be lifted off, making sure that the cork is not likely to pop out. The pressure in the bottle, of 60–70 pounds per square inch, can cause a great deal of damage if it is not kept under control. Light-fittings, spectacles, and valued customers are particularly vulnerable. If the cork shows signs of lifting, it is sensible and correct to remove the cork with the muzzle still in place.

To remove the cork, the bottle should be held firmly at an angle of about 45°, with the cork pointing away from any person or object of value. Still keeping the thumb on the top of the cork, grip the base of the bottle with the other hand and twist the bottle until the cork starts to move. Allow the cork to leave the bottle gently, with no popping sound. Instead, let it sigh! A glass should be conveniently to hand to pour the first drops if the wine effervesces over. This is less likely to happen if the wine is well chilled, as recommended.

Obstinate corks can be removed with a special pair of pliers which can be bought for this purpose. Before pouring, the top of the bottle should be wiped with the napkin. When serving sparkling wine, the traditional and most popular method is to hold the bottle firmly, with the thumb in the hollow at the bottom which is called the *punt*.

The label should be visible to the diner as the wine is poured into tulip-shaped or similar tall glasses (flutes). To wrap the bottle completely in a napkin is incorrect. The photograph shows an acceptable way of using a napkin while leaving the label still visible to the diner. The bottle should then be replaced in the ice-bucket, with the napkin attached, until it is required for topping-up. The wine-waiter must try to anticipate when this will be, to avoid the host having to pour his guests' wine.

# *Tasting Techniques*

The following is a suggested format for a permanent record of your tastings.

| Date tasted | Wine (including shipper) | Vintage or N.V. | Clarity 2 | Colour 4 | Bouquet 4 | Taste 10 | Total 20 | Comments |
|---|---|---|---|---|---|---|---|---|
| | | | | | | | | |

## Points to remember

1. Avoid smoking if you wish to retain a finely tuned palate.
2. Do not eat strongly flavoured foods before tasting.
3. Medications, tablets etc. will interfere with your taste sensations.
4. Perfumes and after-shaves are best avoided if you are to appreciate the bouquet of the wine properly. This is one reason why food service staff are advised not to wear strong perfumes, etc.
5. If you have a cold, or are feeling unwell, you will not perform well when tasting.
6. It is best to taste dry wines before sweet ones, i.e. in the same order in which the wines would be drunk with a meal.
7. Experts usually do not swallow much wine when tasting. It is advisable to have a receptacle on the table to use for the disposal of unwanted wine.
8. Take your time when tasting wine, don't rush it!
9. Use only crystal clear and clean glassware.
10. Pour a generous and adequate sample.
11. Hold the glass by the stem and look through the wine towards the light.
12. Consider first the clarity of the wine. It should be clear and bright. If it is cloudy, this is the first indication that the wine may be out of condition.
13. Assess the colour. A deep colour deserves a high mark on your tasting sheet. A darker colour often, but not always, denotes higher quality. Red wines can vary from almost black to light red. White wines will be somewhere between colourless and a honey or light-brown colour.
14. Take the bouquet of the wine. Swirl the wine around in the glass to release the aroma. Sniff gently over the edge of the glass and try to memorise the impression you get. In time you will be able to identify the different subtle and contrasting sensations provided by different vine varieties. A true wine expert can almost identify the wine at the 'nose' stage.
15. Taste the wine by first swilling the wine around the mouth. Then take a small amount and 'chew' on it, think about it and try to confirm the judgement you made when you took the bouquet. Decide whether the wine is 'thin' (less alcoholic) or full-bodied. Then award marks out of ten.

Award 0 to 2.5 if you would only drink the wine under pressure.
—3 to 5 if you would drink it, but only if someone else is paying for it.
—5.5 to 7.5 if you like the wine and may occasionally buy it.
—8 to 10 if you are enthusiastic about the particular wine.

16. A small amount of cheese, or a cracker biscuit, between wines helps to clear the palate.

Finally, *enjoy* your tasting and try to remember each wine.

*Wine tasting*

# Glassware

In recent years there has been a general move towards standardising the glassware used in popular restaurants, so that less variety needs to be kept, but there are still many traditional glasses available.

**Beer glasses** (1 pint and $\frac{1}{2}$ pint for draught, 12 ozs for bottled beers). Government stamped and lined glasses provide an accurate measure.

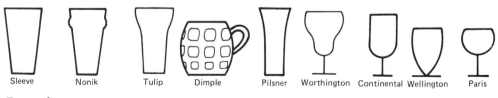

Sleeve    Nonik    Tulip    Dimple    Pilsner    Worthington    Continental    Wellington    Paris

*Beer glasses*

**Spirit glasses** (large enough for a mixer drink to be added i.e. 5 to 7 ozs).

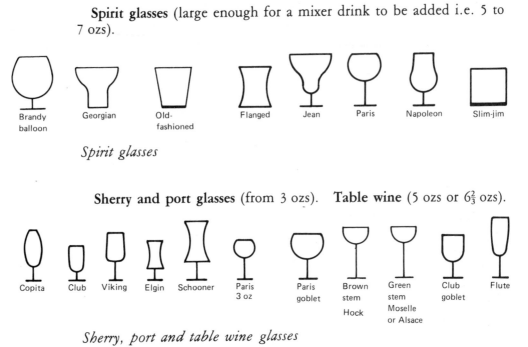

Brandy balloon · Georgian · Old-fashioned · Flanged · Jean · Paris · Napoleon · Slim-jim

*Spirit glasses*

**Sherry and port glasses** (from 3 ozs).   **Table wine** (5 ozs or $6\frac{2}{3}$ ozs).

Copita · Club · Viking · Elgin · Schooner · Paris 3 oz · Paris goblet · Brown stem Hock · Green stem Moselle or Alsace · Club goblet · Flute

*Sherry, port and table wine glasses*

**Liqueur glasses** (usually 1 oz size).

Thistle · Elgin · Jean

*Liqueur glasses*

**Decanters** (cut glass with stopper).
1. Wine decanter (rounded sides).
2. Spirit decanter (square sides).
3. Ship's decanter (broad base).

**Carafes** (do not have stoppers). They are used to serve inexpensive wines. Usual sizes 1 litre, 50 cl, and 25 cl.

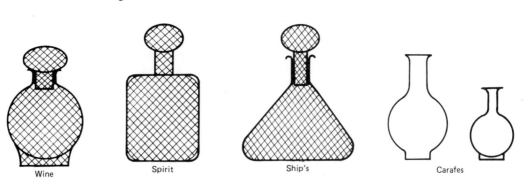

Wine · Spirit · Ship's · Carafes

*Decanters*

# Handling Glassware

For reasons of hygiene, great care must be taken when handling glassware both at the table and at the bar.

Fingers must never come into contact with the rim of the glass. This example is to show that apart from being extremely unhygienic, the method of placing glasses in front of the customer (demonstrated in the diagrams) would be unlikely to bring repeat orders.

It is also recommended that during service all glassware being carried to or from the table should be carried on a salver. Customers' drinks placed on the bar should always be placed on a drip-mat.

It is more convenient to use the right hand to place glasses on the table as they should be placed near the right of the cover, where the customer can pick them up with the right hand. The service and clearing of all glassware from the restaurant table should, wherever possible, be carried out from the right-hand side of the customer.

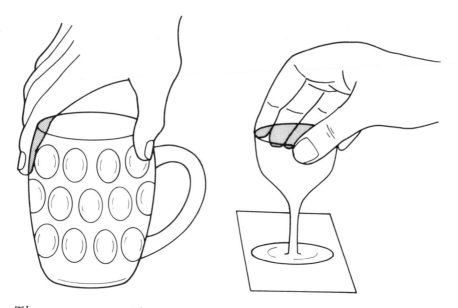

*The wrong way to place down glasses*

Bar staff should make every effort to keep bar and tables clear of empty glasses, and ashtrays should be constantly changed when dirty. A 2-inch (5 cm) paintbrush is quite a useful tool to keep behind the bar to brush out the ashtrays into the waste-bin.

When mixer bottles need to be carried to the restaurant table, the more experienced waiting staff will be seen to carry the baby bottles, with the tops already removed, between the fingers of the left hand, underneath the salver. The reason for this is that the guest is able to see that the spirit which was ordered is in fact in the glass on the salver, and also the mixer bottles can easily be upset when carried upright on the salver. Upon reaching the table it is a simple matter to put down the glass of spirit with the right hand and then, again using the right hand, to pour some of the mixer into the goblet.

All glasses, whether empty or full should be placed down and cleared as shown in the diagrams below. They should always be held by the stem or the base. This rule also applies to beer mugs, which should be held by the base or by the handle.

During the *mise-en-place* (preparation for service) it is usual to carry stemmed glasses with the stems between the fingers of the left hand. This leaves the right hand free to place the glasses on the table. In the right-hand diagram a Paris goblet is being cleared from a drip-mat on the bar. In the left-hand diagram a pilsner lager glass is being cleared from the restaurant table.

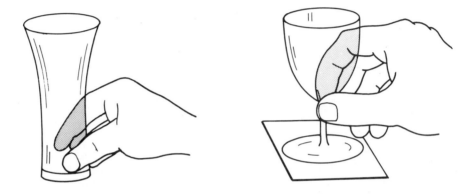

*The right way to place down and clear glasses*

When clean glasses are being cleared from the table at the same time as used glassware, it is a good idea to place the clean glasses on the salver upside-down, so that they are not confused with the dirty ones and do not necessarily go for washing-up. They should, however, be carefully inspected and may need to be washed.

It is always advisable to wash glassware as soon as it has been cleared. If for some reason this is not possible, glasses which have been used for cocktails, liqueurs, or milk, should be filled with water until such time as they can be washed. This prevents the glasses becoming sticky and difficult to wash.

## Manual washing of glassware

Two sinks should be used for this, with a draining board at each side. The dirty glasses should be all placed on one draining board. They should then be swilled, one glass at a time, in the first sink which contains hot water and glass-washing liquid. As soon as the glass has been washed in the first sink, it should be rinsed in the second sink containing hot clean water. The glass should then be placed upside-down on the other draining board until it can be dried with a good quality linen tea-towel. Special attention should be paid to lipstick stains.

# Temperatures for Wine

The ideal storage temperature for wine is somewhere below 50°F (10°C), preferably in cellars deep underground, where it can mature without variation of temperature, undisturbed and, if possible, in darkness.

## Red wine

Most red wines are served *chambre*, i.e. at room temperature, somewhere near 65°F (17°C). To bring red wine up to room temperature from the cold of the cellars, the wine should be left in the room where it is to be served for about four or five hours. If this is not possible, great care must be taken than no artificial means are used to increase the temperature.

**Wine must not be placed near radiators.**

**Wine must not be placed in the hot-cupboard, bain-marie or microwave.**

**Wine must not be placed in or under hot water.**

**Sudden changes of temperature are harmful to wine.**

The only acceptable way of bringing red wine up to room temperature is to pour it carefully into a warmed decanter. The fingers of the hands cupped around the bowl of the goblet will serve the same purpose, but it is not a practical method for the sommelier to consider.

When serving the lighter red wines (Beaujolais, Chinon, etc.), which may sometimes be served cool, it is advisable to ask the customer if the wine is preferred chilled or at room temperature.

## Rosé and white wines

Rosé and white wines should be served chilled. To ensure this the bottle may be left in a refrigerator for more than one hour, or the bottle may be placed in a wine-cooler (ice-bucket) for more than twenty minutes, in ice and water to a level high on the shoulder or neck of the bottle. It is important that the wine-waiter takes the orders in good time to enable this chilling process to be completed. Many establishments have chiller units which maintain the correct temperature. The wine should still be presented in the cooler, so that the wine will stay chilled even when the guests are in no hurry to drink the wine quickly.

The drier white and rosé wines are ideally served at just under 50°F (10°C). Sweeter white wines and champagne are recommended to be served slightly colder, at about 45°F (7°C) to 47°F (8°C).

**White wines and rosé wines must never be placed in the freezer to chill them quickly as this kind of treatment adversely affects the character of the wine.**

The examples given are typical of many similar wines.

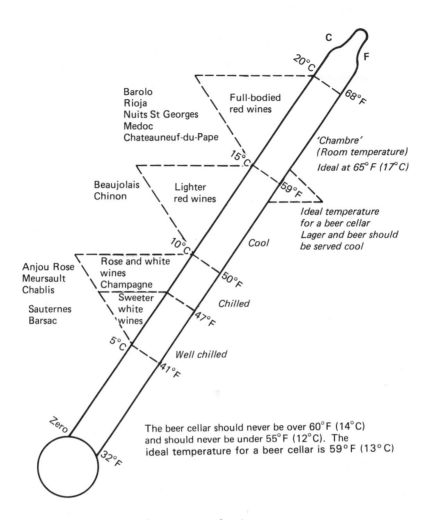

*Temperatures for the service of wine*

# Labelling

## Champagne

Champagne is an area which produces one of the world's finest wines, protected in the UK by laws which forbid the use of the name on any other wine. Recent court action even prevented the use of the word as a description on bottles of sparkling cider.

## Port and madeira

Again, according to UK law, these names can only be used for the fortified wines produced in the respective countries. Many similar wines exist but may not be brought into Britain if they carry on their label the words 'port' or 'madeira'.

## Sherry

With the accession of Spain to the EEC the protection of this wine within the community has been altered by agreement to exclude Australia and South Africa from the shortlist of lands that may call their wine 'sherry'. The new arrangement is that only Spain, Cyprus, and the UK may use the name 'sherry' on their labels if the product is to be sold within the EEC.

## Whisky or whiskey

Whisky can be made anywhere in the world but if it is labelled 'Scotch' then it must be a product of Scotland.

## Brandy

Brandy may be made anywhere but if it is labelled 'cognac' or 'armagnac', the contents of the bottle must be entirely made in the area of France shown on the label.

## Gin

There is no restriction on the countries or areas making gin. Even 'London Dry Gin' can be made anywhere in the world.

## Rum

Following the Royal Commission on Potable Spirits (1909) rum is defined as, 'a spirit distilled from sugar cane products in countries where sugar cane grows'. Countries which are not cane producers must, by British law, include the word 'imitation' (or a translation of it) on the label.

Labels must describe the bottle contents, indicate the country of origin, state the name and head office address of the responsible bottler, and state the nominal volume.

## Wine label language

Labels must avoid giving a false impression or causing confusion.
*Table wine*  Wines of moderate quality which may be a blend of wines from more than one country of the EEC and not less than 8.5 per cent alcohol.
*Vin de Pays*  These French wines are from large district areas of France and are the typical country wines of a region, having an alcoholic strength not less than that specified by the district committee.
*VDQS*  Vins Délimité de Qualité Supérieure are excellent second-quality wines of France from minor districts. They are recognised by a symbol which is black and has the size and appearance of a postage stamp.
*AOC*  Appellation Origine Contrôlée is a geographical guarantee on

*A VDQS stamp*

70

French labels for quality wines that come from a defined area, which may be a large area like the Médoc or a small commune or individual château.

*Landwein* Local German wine from one of fifteen approved landwein regions. It is always dry or semi-dry, comparable with French vin de pays.

*QbA* Qualitätswein bestimmte Anbaugebiete is the title given to quality German wines from specified regions.

*QmP* Qualitätswein mit Prädikat is first quality German wine, the production of which is strictly controlled, which carries the additional 'pradikat' (predicate) or quality designations (e.g. auslese, eiswein etc.).

*DOC* Denominazione di Origine Controllata is the quality status granted to Italian wine districts which have proved to the authorities that their standards of quality maintain a typical regional wine.

*DOCG* Denominazione di Origine Controllata e Garantita. Italian wines labelled in this way are the finest produced in that country. They may not be placed for sale in containers of more than 5 litres.

*Vintage* Literally means 'harvest'. Wines which are from a single year are known as vintage wines. These are exceptional harvests and the year will appear on the label.

*Non-vintage* Wines of poor years are blended with the surplus production of the good years to make an acceptable wine which will bear no year on its label.

Common label terms

| *Term* | *French* | *German* | *Italian* | *Spanish* |
|---|---|---|---|---|
| Dry | Sec | Trocken | Secco | Seco |
| Medium dry | Demi-sec | Halbtrocken | Abbocato | Semi-seco |
| Medium | Moelleux | Lieblich | Amabile | Semi-dulce |
| Sweet | Doux | Süss | Dolce | Dulce |
| Slight sparkle | Pétillant | Spritzig | Frizzante | Petillant |
| White wine | Vin blanc | Weisswein | Vino bianco | Vino blanco |
| Red wine | Vin rouge | Rotwein | Vino rosso | Vino tinto |
| Castle / estate | Château | Schloss | Castello | Domäne |
| Vintage | Vendange | Hauptlese | Vendemmia | Vendimia |

*Mis en bouteille au château* Literally means 'Bottled at the chateau'.

*Classico* The heartland or best viticultural area of the wine regions of Italy.

*Riserva (or Reserva)* Means mature wine of good quality.

*... Villages* As in Mâcon villages, this is a term used for groups of communes in several French areas whose wines are better than average

and which may be blended together and carry an AOC label.

*The 'e' mark* Indicates that the bottler has complied with the EEC liquid directives.

# Decanting

'The separation of wine from its sediment in the bottle.'

Decanting is more common in the United Kingdom than it is in the wine-producing countries of Europe. Old red wines throw a heavy sediment which is known as *lees*. This is made up of deposits of *tannin* and colouring matter which have accumulated, during the long years of maturation, along the side of the bottle as it lay *binned* on its side in the cool dark cellar. Wine bottles should be binned with the label uppermost, or, in the case of vintage port where there may not be a label, with the characteristic white paint-mark on top. Some very old white wines may need to be decanted if a deposit has formed, but this is a fairly rare occurrence.

The sediment in wine is quite harmless, but has an unpleasant gritty texture. It is also indigestible and must not be allowed to cloud the customer's wine. The amount of wine lost after decanting is quite small but in very old vintage wines may amount to a wine-glass full. This can be passed through muslin, or filter paper, and the wine drunk or used in the kitchen.

Decanting is a very delicate operation and the process requires a very steady hand. A candle is the traditional light against which the sediment will show as it is poured into the decanter. Modern light bulbs

*Decanting wine*

could be used equally as well but they lack the mystique of the candle.

Fine crystal decanters complement the fine wines of Burgundy, Bordeaux and the Douro, although decanting may be from one bottle to another.

Vintage port should always be decanted and where sealing wax covers the cork a salver should be placed in position (under the neck of the bottle as it lies in the cradle), to catch the bits as they are cut away. The practice in times past was to break the bottle neck before decanting, using a special pair of tongs which were heated red-hot and used to make a clean cut by being held against the glass.

After wines have been decanted it is important that the original cork and bottle are shown to the diner when the wine is presented. Very old bottles are expected to be very dirty and no attempt must be made to remove the cellar dust.

## Wine cradles

Wine cradles, or decanting baskets, enable the wine staff to keep a bottle of old red wine in the same horizontal position in which it has been carefully stored. Great care must be taken to avoid a swinging motion when carrying a cradled bottle as this causes the wine to become cloudy. The cork should be removed while the bottle is still in its cradle and with the minimum of disturbance. When pouring, the cradle should be held with the hand under the handle, gripping the bottle firmly, and pouring evenly.

*A wine cradle*

Many restaurants use the decanting cradle for the service of all old red wines. This reduces the pouring angle and helps to minimise the backwash of wine from the continual tilting which makes the wine cloudy. But cradles should not be used for service except when there is not enough time to decant or if no decanter is available. There is no point in using a cradle for young red wines which have no deposit. When cradles are used they ought to be dressed with a clean napkin folded neatly under the bottle.

## When to decant

If the wine to be decanted has already become cloudy, it should be left standing in an upright position for forty-eight hours to allow the sediment to settle.

Ideally, a bottle of fine old vintage red wine should be opened and decanted about half an hour before it is to be consumed. Those which are less fine would benefit from one hour before they are needed. Red wines need to breathe, to absorb the oxygen which causes them to mellow and brings out the fruit flavour. Many robust red wines indeed could satisfactorily have the cork removed two hours before service. However, it is not usually possible to prepare wine in this way in the restaurant as the customer's order is not generally known until just before the meal is due to commence.

Decanting may take place in the cellar or in the dining-room, but not until the bottle has been presented to the purchaser in its original cellar condition.

## Decanters and carafes

*Carafes* are used for the service of cheaper wines at the table. They are made of glass and do not have stoppers. *Decanters* are more elegant and are often made of fine crystal. Those which are square-sided are intended for spirits, while the round decanters are for wine. Decanters always have stoppers, often richly cut. Those decanters which are very wide at the base, and taper in triangular fashion towards the neck, are ship's decanters, and remain upright in the bar or on the table in the liner even on the roughest seas.

# Part 4:
# Fortified Wine

*Port*
*Sherry*
*Madeira*
*Aromatised Wines*
*Other Fortified Wines*

# Port

Port wine is produced in Portugal in the mountainous region of the river Douro in the north-east of the country. The wine is made at the *quinta* (property) from any of more than thirty permitted grape varieties grown on steep terraces of *schistous* (brown slate). Most of the grapes are pressed by modern methods of *auto-vinification*, involving large sealed pressure tanks, but some grapes are still footpressed. The vintage takes place in late September.

Port is *fortified* with grape-spirit *early* in the process before all the natural grape-sugar has been converted to alcohol and carbon dioxide gas. This means that port is always sweet, even the so-called 'aperitif' ports. Six months after the harvest, the casks of new wine are taken westwards along the river, by road tanker or by rail, to *Vila Nova de Gaia* at the mouth of the river, opposite Oporto. Until fairly recently this journey was made perilously on sail-boats.

The casks of port, called *pipes*, contain *115 gallons* (523 litres) and are stored in the shippers' *lodges*. Twenty per cent of all port produced is imported into the UK. It is often referred to by the Portuguese as the 'Englishman's wine'.

## Service of port

It is traditional in Britain for the port to be passed around the table by the diners, each person pouring his own wine and handing the decanter to the person on his *left*. The decanter is not placed down on the table at any stage. As soon as the contents are all served the decanter is handed to the waiter, who may replace it with another full of similar wine.

Port makes a very fine accompaniment to hard and semi-hard English cheeses. Stilton and port are almost inseparable. Some restaurants serve Stilton cheese which has had port poured into it and left for the flavours to combine for several days.

> All port wine before exportation is taken to Oporto, to the Instituto do Vinho do Porto, for testing and certification in the laboratories across the river. It is more strictly controlled than most other wine.

## Main types of port wine

**Vintage**   Wine of one year only, bottled after *two* years, but not ready to drink until at least *ten* years old. Vintage port needs to be carefully decanted to separate the wine from its sediment.

**Crusted**   Similar to vintage port but made from a blend of several years. This wine also needs to be decanted as it has a heavy crust.

**Ruby**   A blend of young red ports, left in cask for about *four* years and ready for drinking as soon as bottled.

**Tawny**   A blend of port wines which is left in cask for a longer time, usually between seven and twenty-five years. It is ready for drinking as soon as it has been bottled. During its time in wood it loses its ruby colour and takes on a tawny brown shade.

**White**   White port is made from white grapes and the traditional variety is very sweet, but a white port is now available which is drunk as an aperitif.

**Late bottled vintage**   The wine of one year but bottled after about *five* years and ready for drinking immediately.

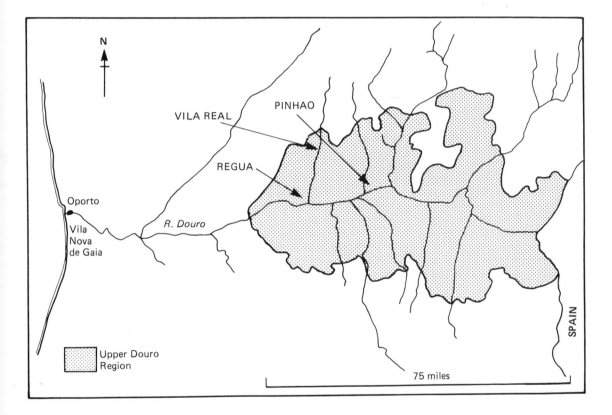

## *The port-wine country*

Only about one-third of the wine made in the Upper Douro is port, the remainder being made into unfortified table wine. Decisions about who may fortify (with grape-spirit), are taken each year by the Casa do Douro depending upon the amount of port required and after consideration of the quality rating of each particular vineyard. Vineyards are graded from A to F. The 'A' vineyards are those with a favourable aspect towards the sun and on the lower slopes, while the 'F' properties would produce wines of lower quality due to location, vine varieties, aspect, and position on the higher slopes.

# Sherry

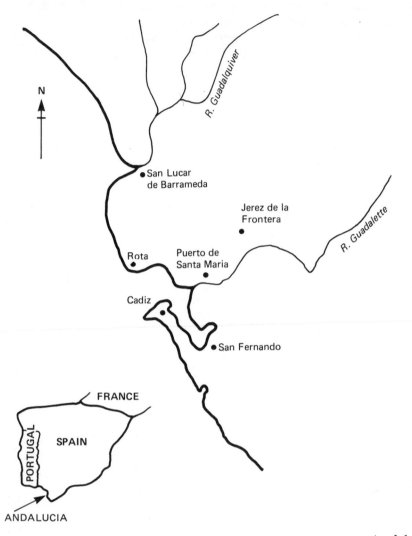

*Andalucia*

The best sherry in the world comes from *Andalucia* in south-west Spain. *Jerez de la Frontera* is the main town. *Sanlúcar de Barrameda* and *Puerto de Santa María* are also important nearer to the coast, the former producing *Manzanilla*, a fine dry *fino* sherry. The finest wine is made from the *Palomino* vine grown on the white chalky *Albariza* soil, squelchy in the short seventy-day rainy season, but solid in summer. All grapes are pressed mechanically.

## Vinification

After the first violent fermentation the progress is slower. In its first year, sherry is in its *Añada* stage and is classified by bouquet. There are two basic sherries: *fino* and *raya*. The *finos* develop after the appearance of an unusual phenomenon. It is *flor*, a yeast crust which forms on the surface of the wine in some casks. The flor has the effect of excluding the oxygen from the wine, keeping it pale in colour. *Fino* sherries may develop in time into *amontillado*. The second basic style of sherry is the coarser *raya* in the casks where *flor* has not occurred. *Rayas* develop into *olorosos*, which are used by the sherry shippers for making into *milk*, *cream*, and *brown* sherries. During its second and third years, sherry rests in the *criaderas* which literally means 'nurseries'. It is still undrinkable.

The warehouses where sherry is made are called *bodegas* and the cask is called a *butt*. A bodega butt is *120 gallons* and a shipping butt is *108 gallons*.

The fermentation of sherry continues in the casks until no sugar is left in the wine. Even the high concentration of sweetness caused by laying the grapes out in the hot sunshine on *esparto grass mats* is converted into alcohol and carbon dioxide gas. All sherry after fermentation is bone dry. Sweetness in the final bottle, if required, is achieved by adding sweetening wine made from the *Pedro Ximineth* grape, usually referred to as *Pedro X*. These grapes are left on esparto mats for two weeks. The dark colour in cream and brown sherry is from boiled Pedro X or Moscatel, called *vino de color*, which is added before bottling. At the end of its third year the sherry wine progresses from the criadera to the shipping *solera*. This is best described as a system of fractional blending. The casks which make up the soleras were first placed in position 120 years ago. During this time the casks have remained in position and no cask has ever been allowed to be less than two-thirds full. Many soleras are built up in tiers, often three or four rows high, but other soleras are made up of a single row of casks at ground level.

*Soleras of sherry casks*

If we use the example of three rows, the solera would operate as follows:
1. Wine for shipping is taken in equal amounts from each cask on the *bottom row*.
2. The *bottom row* is topped up with wine from the *middle row*.
3. The *middle row* is topped up with wine from the *top row*.
4. The *top row* is filled up with wine from the *criadera*.
5. The *criaderas* are topped up with wine from the *anada* stage.

It is acknowledged that when small quantities of the young new wine are put into a cask containing a larger quantity of old wine, the new wine will take on the character of the old, in the same way as a small child starting school quickly learns and changes his pattern of behaviour, although the school itself changes very little because of his arrival.

*Note* Wine is removed from the solera cask by siphon tubes into large jugs, which are used to pour the sherry into funnels on top of the next cask. There are no taps and the transfer is not likely to be undertaken by automation or mechanical means.

Wines which are very similar to the sherries of Andalucia are made in *South Africa*, where a natural *flor* appears on some casks in the same manner as in Spain. Australia and Cyprus also produce good quality wines like the Spanish sherries but without the advantage of a natural *flor*. A cultivated yeast 'flor' is injected into the wine to give pale dry wines similar to the original finos.

Large quantities of wine which bears more than a passing resemblance to sherry is also made in the United Kingdom from imported wine or grape juice. Bristol is the UK centre for the shipping of sherry.

*A copita sherry tasting glass with venencia*

### Fortification of sherry

Sherry is fortified with grape-spirit (brandy) as soon as it has been classified in the *anada* (up to 20 per cent alcohol approximately). Flor, however, will not live in alcohol of more than 16 per cent so *fino* sherries have to be fortified twice: first, up to 14 per cent in the anada; secondly, about 6 per cent more when shipped.

# Madeira

Madeira is a volcanic island rising steeply out of the Atlantic about 400 miles west of Morocco. It was discovered in 1419 for Portugal by Captain Zarco. The name 'Madeira' in Portuguese means 'wood' and probably refers to the thick layer of fertile potash soil which covers the island. This is said to be the result of a great fire that is supposed to have burned for seven years after being started by the first settlers on the densely wooded hillsides.

The mountains reach a height of almost 2,000 metres and are steeply terraced. Many fields are no more than five metres wide. Most of the work has to be carried out by hand as there is little room for animals or tractors to haul machinery. The produce is carried down the steep tracks on the broad backs of the farmers and the materials used in the building of the small farms have been physically carried up the hillsides. Many of the coastal stretches of vineyards have to be approached by boat to collect the grapes as they are virtually inaccessible by land. The range of agricultural produce found in Funchal market includes: avocados, bananas, oranges, mangoes, apples, pears, and runner beans. Potatoes and yams, cabbages and tomatoes, maize, and even sugar-cane are also successfully cropped on Madeira.

The vines are trained over wires or trellises, called 'pergolas', about two or three metres above the ground with a second crop planted on the ground below. The trellis is often extended over the paths leading up to the houses and vines sometimes trail over rooftops.

## Levadas

These are skilfully designed aqueducts constructed to carry water from the areas of heavy rainfall, around the contours of the mountainsides, to the rest of the island. They divide and branch into smaller channels at the lower levels and there are small sluice-gates to direct the water on to each property at certain times, which are very strictly controlled by the island's laws. Owners are allowed to open their gates only twice a week, for short periods, to obtain water.

The larger levadas have pathways alongside them which make very pleasant walkways for tourists to admire the spectacular views.

Vines are grown all over the island, although most of the grapes are carried down to Funchal to be pressed in modern mechanical presses.

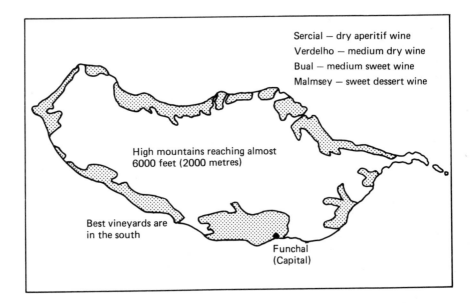

Sercial — dry aperitif wine
Verdelho — medium dry wine
Bual — medium sweet wine
Malmsey — sweet dessert wine

High mountains reaching almost 6000 feet (2000 metres)

Best vineyards are in the south

Funchal (Capital)

*Madeira wines*

### The estufa system

This is a system used in Madeira where the wine undergoes a method of heat-treatment or partial cooking. It developed from a seventeenth-century trade embargo, ordered by King Charles II, forbidding the shipping of *European* wines in English 'bottoms' (flat-bottomed sailing ships) from *European ports* to the American colonies. The British wine merchants quickly realised that, as Madeira was not in Europe, it could conveniently be used as a staging post, and European wines shipped from Funchal to America would not be breaking the embargo. When the wine was taken across the Atlantic its character was substantially changed. The change was thought to be due to the hot sun beating down on the deck of the vessel when it was becalmed during its seven-week voyage.

In order to simulate the conditions of the journey, so that these unusual wines would be available for sale in England without the long voyage to America, the 'estufa' was developed. Large tanks of wine are heated by means of coils of hot pipes of circulating hot water. By this method the merchants are able to alter the nature and taste of the wine by causing the sugars to caramelise. The wine is fortified to about 17° OIML with local spirit. Much Madeira wine is fortified with sugar-cane spirit (rum) but the laws of the EEC forbid the importation of any fortified wines which are not made with grape-spirit (brandy). Estufa wines are not allowed to be exported until they have rested for *thirteen months* after the heat-treatment.

Unfortified table wines are made in the island but are not generally exported to Europe. Some of the fortified wines have been found to have an extremely long shelf life. Madeira dating from 1792 is said to be still drinkable!

*Rainwater* is the name of a particular style of Verdelho madeira.

# Aromatised Wines

Since earliest recorded times wines have been drunk with added herbs, spices and other aromatic ingredients. Hippocras, the aromatised wine of Hippocrates, was spiced and sweetened with honey, and was a favourite drink in England several centuries before the Romans came. In the Middle Ages wines were flavoured with myrrh, myrtle, cloves, ginger, sandalwood, and many other natural ingredients. *Vermouth* is the name given to those flavoured wines which in theory contained *wormwood*, which was first used in Germany in the sixteenth century. Wormwood in German is *wermutt* which was pronounced 'vermutt', hence the origin of the modern name.

Aromatised wines are unlike all other wines in that there are: no vintages; no defined area; and no strict rules for production.

The first modern commercial vermouth was produced in Turin (in Piedmont, north-west Italy) in 1786 by Antonio Carpano. It survives today as *Punt e Mes*. Turin has, over the years, become the centre for the Italian vermouth industry and Marseilles has developed as the main city for the French production. There are certain differences between the French and Italian vermouths.

### French vermouth

This is traditionally *dry* and *white* and made in large quantities from the wines of the *Midi* in the South of France. Most of the French vermouth is subjected to *weathering* in casks which are left out of doors for two years and exposed to climatic variations. There is a loss of about 10 per cent due to evaporation over the two years. The wines are fortified with local brandy up to approximately 19° OIML (33° SIKES).

'Gin and French' was a very popular drink before the Second World War and usually consisted of a measure of gin with a measure of *Noilly Prat* or similar dry French vermouth.

### Italian vermouth

This is traditionally *sweet* and *red* and made from wines brought from all over Italy to Turin for processing. The Italian vermouths are not usually weathered and the sweetness comes from added *caramel*. The wines are ready for sale much more quickly than the French vermouths. Local Italian brandy is used for fortification.

'Gin and It' i.e. gin and sweet martini, was also much drunk in England prior to 1939.

The market has become very confusing as Italy now produces French-style vermouths and France produces similar wines to those originally made in Italy.

Vermouths, particularly the drier ones, are excellent *aperitifs* and are considered by many people to be *beneficial to health*.

# Other Fortified Wines

After considering port, sherry, madeira and vermouth, attention must be turned to other wines of the world to which brandy is added.

### Angelica

A sweet white fortified wine from California made from the black *Mission* grape with skins excluded from the fermentation, similar in taste to white port.

### Californian Tokay

This has no connection with Hungarian Tokay. It is made by adding local port and sherry to Angelica.

### Commandaria (Commandarie St John)

A lightly fortified brown dessert wine named after the ancient order of crusading knights, and made on the slopes of the Troodos mountains in Cyprus since the twelfth century. (See page 41.)

## Malaga

This is a white, lightly fortified wine from south-east Spain. It is sweetened with evaporated unfermented grape must which has been cooked over an open fire until syrupy and dark brown in colour. Muscatel and Pedro X wines are used.

## Marsala

This is a fortified white wine from Palermo in Sicily. It has a burnt sugar taste due to the addition of evaporated grape-juice mixed with fresh juice and brandy. There is also a dry variety called 'Virgen'. Marsala as we know it today was developed by John Woodhouse in 1773, an Englishman who made money by selling the wine to Lord Nelson's fleet.

## Moscatel de Setubal

This is a lightly fortified white wine from near Lisbon in Portugal. It is aged in wood for up to twenty-five years.

## Pineau des Charentes

Coming from the Cognac district of France, this originally surplus wine was mixed with grape-juice to give a lightly fortified sweet white wine.

## Sherry and port-type wines

These are made in many countries, including Australia, South Africa, USSR, California, Canada, Britain and Cyprus.

## Tarragona

This is a sweet red fortified wine from Catalonia in north-east Spain.

## Vins Doux Naturels

VDN or 'Natural Sweet Wine' is French sweet red and white fortified wine, especially in the regions of Rivesaltes, Banyuls, Frontignan, Rasteau, and Beaumes-de-Venise. The wine is made by adding brandy to half-fermented grape-juice. It is made mainly from the *Muscat* grape-variety.

Fortified wines in France are called 'Vins de Liqueur'.
In Germany, they are 'Likörwein'.
In Spain—'Vino Generoso'.
In Italy—'Vino di Lusso'.
Fortified wines are protected from bacterial attack by the high level of alcohol and this was probably the reason for the first fortification.

84

# Part 5:

# Eating and Drinking

*Wine and Food*
*Shellfish*
*Meat*
*Game*
*Sweets and Desserts*

# Wine and Food

Well-prepared food and good service are always appreciated by customers, but the source of the greatest satisfaction to most guests is the combination of good food and well-chosen wines. It is important that at all times the customer is allowed complete freedom in his own choice of wines. What may be to his liking may well be frowned upon by the connoisseur of fine wines, but the customer must never be allowed to feel that his choice of wine displeases the austere wine butler.

Over the years 'experts' have made up their minds which wines go best with different foods, but many eminent wine drinkers have scorned their advice and committed the unforgiveable 'sin' of drinking red wine with fish or sweet white wine with beef. There is no reason why a customer should not do likewise, but it is also important for the wine-waiter to know his wines and to be ready and willing to give advice when asked.

A few general rules are set out below which will help the inexperienced waiter in those first consultations with the diner or when discussing the wines to accompany a formal dinner function.

1) *The aperitif*, known as the pre-prandial drink, should be a *dry* wine. It is intended to stimulate the taste buds to prepare the way for the food to follow. Aperitifs should never be sweet and, although many people order a gin and tonic before a meal, spirits act unkindly on the salivary glands. Dry or medium dry sherry, dry vermouths, and Sercial Madeira are all excellent aperitifs.

2) *The early courses* are best served with a dry white or dry rosé wine.

3) Where possible, keep the *fine, expensive wines* until later in the meal.

4) Try to accompany *national dishes* with wines from that country if possible, e.g. pasta is complemented by red Italian wine.

5) *Shellfish* and *fish* dishes are accompanied best by dry white wines.

6) *Red meats* (beef, lamb, etc.) are best with red wines.

7) *White meats* (pork, veal, etc.) please most with medium white wine.

8) *Game dishes* need robust red wines to counter the heavy flavour.

9) *Sweets* and *desserts* are served at the end of the meal and it is most appropriate to recommend sweet wines. An expensive luxury sweet deserves a fine quality wine and fortunately a great variety of sweet white wines are available. Sweet wines from the Loire are especially delightful with desserts containing fruit.

10) *Port* is the traditional drink to accompany *Stilton* cheese, even to the extent of pouring old port into a whole mature Stilton and serving the customer with the scooped-out enriched cheese several days later. Most *cheeses* combine harmoniously with port or other sweet red wines.

11) *Brandy* or *liqueurs* make a fitting end to a meal, drunk slowly with *coffee* and perhaps a large cigar. Opportunities for selling are enormous!

# Shellfish

Wines to accompany shellfish are usually *white* and *dry*. This combination of food and wine is acceptable to the diner, as the fresh and acidic flavour of the wine makes a fine balance with the oily or light texture of the fish.

Some of the best examples of dry white wines are:

*Champagne brut*
*Chablis* (Burgundy)
*Meursault* (Burgundy)
*Pouilly-Fuissé* (Burgundy)
*Entre-deux-Mers* (Bordeaux)
*Alsace* (most Alsace wines)
*Sancerre* (Loire)
*Muscadet* (Loire)
*Frascati* (Italy)
*Steinwein* (Germany)

Any of these wines could also be chosen to accompany other fish dishes.

If the fish or shellfish dish is prepared in a sweet sauce then a slightly sweeter wine would be more appropriate. For example: Château Olivier (Graves) or a German hock.

Whelk

Shrimps and prawns

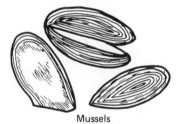

Mussels

Dry rosé wine would be an excellent choice with salmon.

Always remember, however, that the customer who chooses what you consider to be a 'wrong' wine is entitled to his opinion and it should be served with the same professional expertise as the 'acceptable' wine.

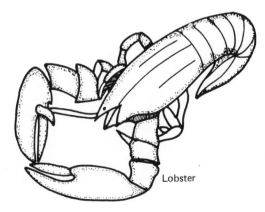

Lobster

# Meat

To accompany *lamb* and *beef*, red wine of all varieties is considered to be suitable. For example, wines such as:

*Claret* (Bordeaux red)
*Burgundy* (any red Burgundy)
*Bardolino* (Italy)
*Chianti* (Italy)
*Valpolicella* (Italy)
*Chinon* (Loire)
*Bull's Blood* (Hungary)
*Zinfandel* (California)

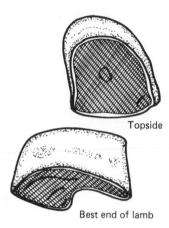

Topside

Best end of lamb

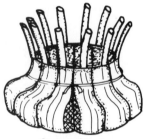

Crown of lamb

*Pork* and *veal* dishes deserve a wine which is of medium character and white. German wines, especially the hocks, pair well with these foods. *Liebfraumilch* is an example of a popular wine which is unlikely to raise criticism. Other suitable wines would include: Graves (white) such as *Château Olivier, Entre-deux-Mers* (Bordeaux) and *Soave* (Italy).

Some people prefer light red wines with white meats when they are roasted, but it is important to remember that whatever the customer chooses is the right wine.

*Poultry* (chicken and turkey). Light red wines will prove most successful with roast poultry, excluding game. For example:

*Beaujolais* (Burgundy)
*Chinon* (Loire)

*Cold chicken* and *turkey* are accompanied well by light, fresh, even pétillant white wines. Drier rosé wines would be equally suitable.

# Game

A selection of wines which would best complement game dishes are listed below. They are all full-bodied and red.

*Rhône red wines:*
St. Joseph
Hermitage
Châteauneuf-du-Pape
*Burgundy (north):*
Nuits St. Georges
Gevrey-Chambertin
*Claret:*
Médoc or Graves
*Italy:*
Barolo or Chianti Classico.
*Spain:*
Rioja or La Mancha

Deer
(Venison)

Mallard

Hare

    These wines all benefit from being opened about one hour before service if possible.

    There are many other wines from various parts which would go equally well with game dishes. These robust wines are particularly suitable because they counter the highly flavoured meats. But the same wines could be served satisfactorily with domesticated fowl, ducks, geese, guinea fowl etc.

    *Note* Glasses of red wine should be filled to just above half-full to enable the diner to appreciate fully the bouquet.

# Sweets and Desserts

Many good meals can be spoiled because insufficient thought has been given to the final phase, and the sweet course can sometimes be a bit of an anti-climax. But whatever the choice of sweet course or dessert, the good wine-waiter will try to offer tactful but helpful advice to enhance the customer's enjoyment of the meal. Thus with the sweet course, the recommendation should be from the following list.

Sweet white wines from the *Loire* Valley are especially good with fruit dishes, fresh fruit salads etc. *Sauternes* or neighbouring wines from other Bordeaux areas (*Cerons, Loupiac, St. Croix du Mont*) or the *Graves* region and *Monbazillac* from just outside the Bordeaux region can be recommended.

*German* sweet white wines such as the *Auslese*, *Beerenauslese*, or the ultimately luscious *Trockenbeerenauslese* are good with desserts.

*Italian* sweet wines, such as *Locorotondo*, are also very acceptable.

Sparkling wines are excellent with the sweet course, *rich champagne* in particular or, of course, the Italian Asti Spumante.

It is best not to recommend any wine with chocolate desserts as the chocolate masks the delicacy of the wine, just as wine cannot be appreciated if it is served with *any* highly flavoured items such as *curry*, or hors d'oeuvres in *vinegar*.

*Cheese* and wine can combine together in many different and delightful ways. *Blue-veined* cheeses are best served with a light red wine such as *claret* while cream cheeses seem to satisfy more if served with a sweetish white or rosé wine, such as *Vouvray* (white Loire) or *Anjou* (rosé Loire). *Port* and *Stilton* are inseparable, and a full red would best suit *cooked curd* cheeses and the *hard* cheeses of the UK.

# Part 6:

# Bar-work

*Bar Equipment*
*Bar Preparation*
*Bar Service*
*Taking Orders*
*Cocktails*
*Cocktail Equipment*

# Bar Equipment

A well organised bar is easy to recognise. The first and lasting impression is one of well-being and warmth. At the planning stage the equipment will have been sited in the most convenient positions for ease and efficiency of service and bar staff will be happy in such an environment. The furnishings and decor will encourage people to return.

Great care should be taken that all items of equipment are left clean at the end of each session ready for the next shift. *Knives* for cutting fruit should be left near to the *cutting board* after washing. The board itself should be washed quickly and not left in the water to lose its shape. *Bottle openers* of several kinds are required. *Crown cork openers*, for removing beer bottle tops, are generally attached to the bar top and have a plastic or metal container which catches the tops as they fall. These should be emptied at the end of every service and cleaned to prevent a beery smell. *Wine bottle cork removers* are available which may be attached to the bar or a table top. They are especially useful for the banquet trade when a large number of bottles need to be opened in a short time away from the customer's table.

Every member of staff should have their own personal *lever extractor corkscrew* (waiter's friend). *Butterfly cork removers* and *continental two-way twist openers* are very efficient but too bulky to carry in the pocket. The latter is especially useful for taking the cork out of a heavily sedimented bottle of wine while it is in the wine cradle prior to decanting. A *broken cork extractor* should be available in the bar.

*Funnels* and *strainers* may be needed when decanting or making cocktails. *Citrus squeezers* vary from small glass models to others which are made of metal and can be attached to a table surface.

*Cooling equipment* requires a substantial amount of space in the bar.

*A cooling shelf*

*In-line coolers* may be installed which lower the temperature of the beer as it passes through. They are located between the cask or keg and the service pump. They are especially important when the bar has no cool underground cellar. *Cooling shelves* are manufactured which hold between 20 and 120 bottles of lager, beer, fruit juices or minerals. Some bars have a *shallow display tub* containing ice on the bar top to hold bottles of lager. *Ice-making equipment* is essential close to the bar area for cocktail making and for inclusion in many drinks such as vermouth, gin and tonic etc. *Lidded insulated containers* of ice should be placed on the bar top, complete with *ice-tongs* or a *dessert spoon*.

*Optics* are measuring units made of glass and metal. They are fitted on top of bottles of wines and spirits which are then inverted and supported in an upside-down position. An accurate measure of liquor is dispensed when a glass is pushed firmly upwards under the release valve.

*Jigger measures* are used when an optic is not in position. The smaller measure, usually a 'six-out', is used for a single portion of spirit, while the larger one, a 'three-out' size, is used for either a double spirit or a single measure of fortified wine (port, sherry, vermouth or madeira).

*Siphons* of soda-water should always be available on the bar for use by the customer or the bar staff. *Trays* and *salvers* are used to carry drinks to the table and for clearing glasses from the tables. *Coasters* are used in some hotels when the wine bottle is left standing on the table. A *side-plate* should be used if a coaster is not available.

*Cocktail shakers* and *mixing glasses* are necessary if cocktails are offered for sale. *Blenders* are important if fresh fruit is to be used as an ingredient. A power point near to a convenient work surface is required so that a blender can be left in place, along with an *electric kettle* for use when making hot toddies, etc. *Bar spoons* (known as muddlers) are needed for stirring cocktails. *Wine coolers* and *ice-buckets* are usually kept in the dispense bar, or wherever the white and rosé wines are stored, or in the restaurant.

*Optics and measures*

*Table top ice-crushers* are used to grind the ice cubes into snow ice for use in frappés, cocktails, etc. They are usually manually operated but electrical crushers are available.

*Glass-washing equipment* should be sited in the bar if space is available. Many different systems are manufactured but whichever type is installed, a temperature of at least 170°F is needed to render bacteria harmless. A frequent water change must also take place. *Dispensers* of *sterilising fluid* may be fitted to taps for sink-washing and also for automatic feeding into electrical glass-washers.

A wide range of *glassware*, including *decanters, carafes*, and *water jugs,* with a good back-up stock for banquets and function trade, should be within easy serving reach of the bar-person.

A selection of *ashtrays* for use on the bar tables, preferably fairly wide and of heavy material, as well as a 4 cm dry *paintbrush,* for use when cleaning them, should be purchased. A *bottle basket, skip, bin* or *crates* must be in place for bottle disposal.

# Bar Preparation

## Morning duties

The atmosphere and general calm which customers enjoy in a bar or restaurant is largely due to the careful preparation which went on in the period before morning opening time. Early morning cleaning duties must be carried out thoroughly to give the area an attractive shine and appearance for the rest of the day. Glasses from the night before should have been washed after closing and all items likely to leave a lingering beery smell should have been removed before finally locking up. Empty bottles should be in the store awaiting the cellar-man's morning sort-out, when he will separate the beer and mineral bottles into crates according to their size. Wine and spirit bottles are consigned to the rubbish disposal point and crown cork bottle tops are discarded. Ashtrays should also have been brushed out into a suitable receptacle and washed. The morning team can then concentrate upon the preparation duties which include:

1. Completing the requisition for bar stocks for the whole day's trading. This is usually required by the cellar department before 09.30 to give time for the issues to be made before opening time.

2. Vacuuming the carpet areas and polishing floors as required. Some bar areas will probably need wet-mopping. Chairs may be placed on the tables during cleaning.

3. Dusting should be carried out systematically.

4. Unlocking and checking that the toilets are clean.

5. Cleaning one area of the bar shelves thoroughly on each day of the week, so that over the seven-day period every part of the bar receives special attention.

6. Requisitioning whatever food items may be required from the stores. Nuts and crisps should be spaced on the bar in clean bowls and lemon and orange slices arranged conveniently in the service area. Cherries, cherry-sticks, parasols and drip-mats should be obtained and placed in position. Stocks of cleaning materials should be replenished.

7. Wiping and polishing bar and table tops where appropriate.

8. Collecting clean linen in good time before service.

9. Positioning the new stock, when it arrives, on the shelves in the bar behind the bottles which are already there. Labels should always face the customer with each bottle wiped clean as it is put in place. Old stock is pulled to the front and the new stock arranged behind.

10. Checking that an adequate supply of ice is available.

11. Ensuring that the float contains enough of each coin denomination to meet the likely needs of the day.

12. Positioning cocktail equipment where it will be needed.

13. Considering whether the customers will be warm enough in the bar. Approximately 60°F (15°C) is about right at opening time.

14. Checking that all optics are in working order.

15. Attending to the beer casks in the cellar by removing the spile from the shive (see page 109) just before service time and turning on the beer taps. If a cellar-man is employed, he will attend to this aspect. A small sample of each beer should be tasted. This last point should be verified with the supervisor in case he wishes to carry out this task himself.

16. Arranging whatever display you consider appropriate for the day to help you to increase your sales. It may be a neat sales aid, featuring one particular drink, or it may be a notice which steers the customer's thoughts towards a certain cocktail or a special dish from the food area.

17. Polishing the glassware, an aspect of work which *can* win friends and influence people! Sparkling glassware is good for business. Always use a clean linen glass-cloth. Handle the glass as little as possible, and hold it up to the light to check that it is clean.

18. Place jugs of fresh water on the bar.

19. Open the doors at the authorised time.


## Late duties

Closing duties at the end of the day, known as 'fermeture', should be completed in the following order, after having accompanied the last guest to the door and watched them leave the premises:

1. Lock and bolt the door securely at the authorised time.

2. Check and clear the tills and pay the takings in to the reception department or lock them in the safe.

3. Enter the amount of takings on the bar summary sheet.

4. Remove all empty bottles from the bar.

5. Replace spiles in the shives of the beer casks in the cellar and turn off the beer taps.

6. Open the windows to allow the fresh air in to dispel smoke.

7. Collect all glasses and ashtrays from the bar tables.

8. Check that no one is hiding in the toilets and lock the doors.

9. Brush out the ashtrays with a 4 cm or 5 cm paintbrush.

10. Make the bar ready for early cleaning the next morning by placing the chairs on the tables.

11. Start a requisition list of known items of stock which will be required the next day. This will save time in the morning when different staff may be on duty. The list will finally be completed by the next day's morning team.

12. Put bar swabs into a plastic bucket containing a weak solution of bleach until the following morning.

13. Wash all glassware. If a mechanical glasswasher is used it could be set in motion much earlier whilst other tasks were being attended to.

14. Disconnect electrical equipment, except for tills and refrigeration or cooling cabinets, by removing the plugs from the sockets.

15. Pull down and secure all grills, hatches and windows and place any keys in the safe.

16. Turn off all the bar lights and lock internal doors.

# Bar Service

If you work in a popular bar you can expect to have customers from the moment when you first pull back the bolt at opening time until you see them off the premises at closing time. The atmosphere may be smoky and the noise may be unpleasantly loud. You may be expected to carry on numerous conversations with customers at different parts of the bar about subjects in which you have very little, if any, interest. At the same time you will be trying to concentrate on recalling from your mind all the practical skills you have aquired, customers' names, prices of drinks, etc. and there will be some who will expect you to remember what they drank on their last visit several months before! It is little wonder that some busy bartenders forget to smile!

There are also rules to be obeyed about what *not* to do when serving behind the bar. *Smoking* is forbidden under the Food Hygiene Regulations. Customers who are smoking can lean over the bar, but the operative who is serving cannot smoke as they are in what is regarded as a food area. Alcoholic drinks are foods.

*Eating* behind the bar is not illegal, but it is impolite and it is not possible to serve and eat at the same time. *Drinking* may be allowed by the management but no bar-person can operate properly after drinking alcohol. If you are offered drinks, it is best to refuse politely by saying that you are not allowed to drink on duty, but you may do so after closing time. Monies which are paid over in this way by the customer should be kept separate so that the supervisor will understand that it was a 'tip'.

Wherever possible bar staff should face the customer when dispensing drinks. When pouring a bottle of beer, the label should be towards the purchaser. The bottle should be held at an angle of 45° in one hand and the glass at a similar angle in the other. Bottled beer should be poured gently at first, with the bottle raised slightly higher as the glass gets fuller. This brings the head of froth to the top of the glass and makes the drink more presentable.

Non-pasteurised beers, like bottled Guinness, Worthington White Shield, and Bass Red Triangle, should be poured carefully, and a small amount left in the bottle because of the sediment it contains.

When serving lager and lime, the lime should be poured into the glass after the beer because of its density. In shandies, always remember

*Pouring bottled beer*

to put the lemonade in the glass first as there is less frothing when the beer is added.

All drinks served should be placed on a drip-mat.

Jigger measures used for the service of spirits and fortified wines must be rinsed each time after use or placed upside down on the *jigger drainer*.

The fastest selling lines of bottled beers should be located near the point of sale, i.e. the centre of the bar, to prevent extra walking and to save time. Each bar-person should have his own fully equipped section, although it may be necessary for everyone to use the same till.

Try to recognise your customers when they enter and if possible greet them by name, afterwards referring to them as 'sir' or 'madam'.

Avoid chatting too much with one customer, but if there is a lonely drinker you must give him as much attention as possible without neglecting your other duties. You may be able to get another customer to join in a three-way conversation, which will start them talking to each other.

In a busy bar I maintain that one bar-person should be able to cope effectively with twenty-five drinkers. This does not mean that, if there are more than that number in the bar, another member of staff will be brought in. I have known many cases where one barman was expected to serve ninety people. But service inevitably gets slower and, if they have to wait for their drinks, people get irritable and go elsewhere.

It is inadvisable for bar-tenders to get involved in discussions about politics, religion, race relations, the brewery, or people in the locality. The reason is simple: customers may be lost if they dislike your point of view. They may gossip and cause others to leave your bar. You must never allow yourself to get drawn into an argument; in fact, you will probably find your role will often be that of peacemaker to bring arguments to an end.

If you hear rumours, or 'local news', keep it to yourself. Be tactful, especially if you know that the customer is with someone else's spouse! If the telephone rings and someone asks to speak to a customer in the bar, ask the customer first if they are in the bar! They may not want that information to be conveyed to the person on the line.

Avoid the temptation to get involved in 'wagers' or betting with people in the bar, and remember that it is illegal to give credit to drinkers for alcohol served on licensed premises.

As a final point, always remember to keep foodstuffs covered in the bar and wash your hands frequently.

Working in a bar is never dull or monotonous. You will continually meet interesting and extraordinary folk, each with their own personalities and stories to tell. The wit and repartee in a public bar *can* be sparkling and, while you may be involved in the humour, you must never lose sight of your purpose, i.e. to encourage the customers to partake of the goods and services the establishment offers. It is not in your interests for them to get drunk, and they are more likely to return if they enjoy their evening.

Always maintain the highest standards of service, and work with your colleagues to make your bar a place where the public can expect friendship, warmth and efficiency.

# Taking Orders

### At the table

The short time taken to record a customer's order is the best opportunity to increase potential sales. First of all, when the guests arrive, and are seated at the table, the sommelier must quickly decide who is the host in the party. Good waiters can, by natural instinct, identify the host immediately. The host is the person responsible for paying the bill and he will be making sure that everything is in order for his guests. He will be the one who introduces people to each other if they are strangers. He probably reserved the table in his own name and will usually be the last one to sit down. The host may not be the oldest in the party and, although I have used the male pronoun here, the host can be a man or a woman.

*The beverage list* should be clean, with no obvious price alterations. It should be presented to the host from his right. At this point I consider it to be important for the wine-waiter to leave the table for a short time while the guests consider their choice. They may wish to decide quietly whether or not they can afford to buy wine! Wine lists could be taken to other tables during this time.

'May I take your order, please, sir', is a good phrase to use when you return to the table. Assistance may be needed to enable the diners to select the most suitable beverage in relation to the foods chosen. If time allows, it may even be possible to sell an aperitif while they are waiting for their first course. The sommelier must know his wines and also the likes and dislikes of his regulars.

The *check-pad*, used to record alcoholic beverage sales, is normally of coloured paper. The sommelier should record clearly the necessary details as follows: table number and number of covers (and room number if the diner is a resident); the beverage required, which will be recorded as the Bin no. in the event of wine being ordered, i.e. $1 \times 32$, or $\frac{1}{2} \times 17$ etc.; the price of the item; the waiter's initials; and the date.

The total price of the items on the check should be shown in a circle thus – ⟨5.68⟩. Modern restaurant billing machines automatically record the correct price on the bill, which saves the wine-waiter from having to make any additions.

When the order has been taken, the original and duplicate checks should be separated. The top copy is taken by the commis to the dispense bar, while the duplicate copy should be handed to the cashier.

*Function beverages* are often chosen in advance by the organisers or, alternatively, each waiter may take separate orders from the diners at the respective tables, collecting cash and giving change when they serve the wine. One of the most complicated orders is when a large party requires an assortment of liqueurs. Clear concentration and a good memory are an asset. Some waiters devise methods to help them, such as arranging the glasses on the salver in the same positions as the diners are seated around the table.

### In the bar

Most bar staff work without any form of written checks or control of drinks served. Modern computer systems require the appropriate button to be pressed every time a sale is made. This maintains a complete record of all stocks sold and unsold. But few bars have computers and many staff are happier if they can write down the prices so that, if they are interrupted, they can continue without becoming confused. However, writing things down does waste valuable serving time!

When serving drinks, try to add up the prices in your head as you serve each one—remembering the complications of doubles and singles, half pints, shandies (which may involve a separate calculation), and additions of lemonade, lime-juice, orange squash, etc., which may be priced at so much a 'splash'. Be prepared for the character in the bar who comes up for a large round of drinks and, when you are half-way through, forgets what else he wanted and has to return to his party. This is when a pad and a biro are most useful. You can jot down the amount served up to that point and turn your attention to another customer, continuing the addition when the original person returns a few minutes later to complete his order.

*Cigarettes* and *tobacco* sales are recorded separately in some restaurants and hotels, as also are food sales in some bars. This is done so that the analysis of sales can be correctly recorded for accounting purposes. The necessary forms will be beside the till in places where this is considered important. Modern electronic tills have separate item buttons which make the necessary analysis.

Remember that bar sales will increase if glasses are removed from tables and bar tops as soon as they become empty, and a smiling, 'Can I get you another drink, madam?' usually leads to a positive response.

## Methods of payment

*Cash* is the most common method of payment in the bar. Count the change out to the customer by continuing to add upwards from the price of the drinks to the amount tendered. Take care not to hand out change over the drinks as it is very easy to drop a coin accidentally into a glass. Large denomination banknotes should be left in a visible position until the customer has accepted their change in case they mistakenly think they gave you a £20 note when in fact it was only £10.

*Cheques* are more likely to be used in payment in the restaurant. Customers who wish to write a cheque in payment may do so; but the staff must scrutinise the cheque very carefully and only accept it if it is accompanied by a banker's authorisation card, which guarantees that payment up to £50 is in order. The waiter or bar-person should check that the signatures match, and write the card number on the back of the cheque along with the customer's address.

*Credit cards* are probably the simplest form of payment. The customer simply signs against his transaction on a special form for the particular card used. Payment is made by the credit card company, while the diner pays for his meal on his monthly credit card account.

*Residents* who purchase food or wine in the restaurant, or drinks in the bar, may have the amount of money owing placed on their account which they pay on departure. The service personnel must ask if the person is a resident. If so, the room number must be placed on the top of the check which the resident must sign. Many companies have monthly accounts.

# Cocktails

This the exotic section of the drinks market.

Because of the increased demand for fun and change in the drinking habits of the public, it is essential that bar staff keep themselves up-to-date and conversant with modern trends.

Countless stories abound concerning the origins of what we now know as cocktails. One story says it was *Betsy Flanagan*, the widow of a revolutionary officer in the war of American Independence in 1779, who stole her neighbour's chickens and decorated the glasses in the bar with the cock's tail feathers. Another talks of a mixed drink called *Coquetel*, originating in Bordeaux and drunk by French officers in George Washington's army. Or cocktails may even have originated from *Coquetiers*, which were mixed drinks served in eggcups in cold weather to his customers by a New Orleans chemist. All these are possible. Even the old English term *Cock-ale* could have been the forebear of our present term 'cocktail'. Cock-ale was the mixed drink which was drunk after a cock-fight in eighteenth-century England, the mixture containing the same number of drinks as there were feathers left in the winning cockerel's tail. In Mexico the locals drank mixtures which were stirred with a wooden root called 'cola de gallo' (cock's tail).

*A cocktail bar*

The cocktail era really started to emerge when the first book of cocktails was produced in 1860 by an American barman called *Jerry Thomas*. This was followed in 1882 by *Harry Johnson's Bartender's Manual*. The first British publication was a 1930s magazine called 'The Bartender', to which *Harry Craddock*, of the Savoy Hotel, London, was a regular contributor.

The peak in cocktail popularity was reached between 1920 and 1937. These years have been described as the 'cocktail age' and correspond with the years of *Prohibition* in the United States (1919 to 1935). During these years the sale and manufacture of alcohol in the USA was forbidden. Instead of controlling the abuse of alcohol, the restrictions led to organized disregard of the law. Extortion and gangland warfare, the rise and fall of the notorious Al Capone and similar underworld leaders, and wholesale and flagrant production and sale of 'moonshine' whisky and other illegal and harmful liquors, were all results of the misguided legislation. These unwholesome alcohols could be cleverly disguised by mixing and shaking with non-alcoholic ingredients.

*The United Kingdom Bartender's Guild* was formed in 1934, and Harry L. Craddock, mentioned earlier, was the first President. Its aims have always been to create a higher standard of efficiency, and to promote better understanding and goodwill among cocktail bartenders throughout the world.

Cocktails may be: *stirred, shaken,* or *poured (built)*. The decision about which of these methods to use depends on several factors:
1. If the cocktail contains a cloudy ingredient, such as fresh cream, egg yolk, lemon juice, orange juice, or similar opaque items, then it should be *shaken*.
2. If the ingredients are all clear, then the cocktail should be *stirred*.
3. If the drinks involved are of different specific gravities, and the bartender wishes to keep the layers separate, then the cocktail should be *built* (poured).

Almost all cocktails should be drunk cold. The purposes of the mixing glass and the cocktail shaker is to bring the temperature of the mixture rapidly down by speedy movement in contact with ice. Five or six ice cubes are usually sufficient to achieve the desired result.

Many modern cocktail bars include amongst their equipment a cocktail blender. A blender is most useful when fresh fruit is an ingredient in the drink, for example, Banana Daiquiri and Saronno Fruit Whirl.

## Some popular cocktails

**Alexander**   A shaken cocktail, served in a small cocktail glass.
   1/3 brandy, 1/3 Crème de Cacao, 1/3 fresh cream.
**Americano**   A stirred cocktail, served in a wine glass.
   1/3 campari, 2/3 sweet vermouth. Top up with soda-water and add a twist of lemon.
**Bloody Mary**   A shaken cocktail, served in a wine glass or a slim-jim.
   1/3 vodka, 2/3 tomato juice, angostura bitters, juice of half a lemon. Many bartenders stir this mixture in the glass in which it is to be served. Worcestershire sauce is sometimes added.
**Bronx**   A shaken cocktail, served in a small cocktail glass.
   1/2 dry gin, 1/6 dry vermouth, 1/6 sweet vermouth, 1/6 orange juice.
**Champagne Cocktail**   A poured cocktail, served in a champagne glass or goblet.
   One lump of sugar saturated with angostura bitters, a small amount of brandy. Top up with iced champagne and add a slice of orange.
**Royal Clover Club**   A shaken cocktail, served in a double cocktail glass.
   1/4 gin, 1/4 grenadine, 1/4 lemon juice, one egg yolk.
   Cocktails containing egg should be throughly shaken to cause the egg to froth. Pour with an 'up and down' movement.

**John Collins**   A shaken *or* poured cocktail, served in a tall glass, i.e. Wellington or slim-jim.

Gin (or other spirit), sugar, juice of half a lemon and some egg-white. Shake well and strain into the tall glass. Fill with soda-water and decorate with a slice of lemon. Take care not to use too much gin. Approximately 1½ fl oz is sufficient. The pouring method involves placing all the ingredients, including the soda-water, into the glass, and stirring.

**Cuba Libre**   A poured cocktail, served in a tumbler or taller glass.

Rum plus the juice of half a lime, topped up with coca-cola. Some bartenders half fill the glass with crushed ice before pouring.

**Rum Fizz**   A shaken *or* poured cocktail, served in a tall glass, i.e. Wellington.

Rum, barspoon of sugar, juice of half a lemon—shake and strain into the tall glass. Top up with soda-water and add an ice-cube.

**Frappé**   A poured cocktail, served in a flute wine glass.

Fill the flute glass with crushed ice and pour a liqueur over the ice to colour it. Several different colours may be used, poured from different sides of the glass. Serve with two short straws.

**Harvey Wallbanger**   A shaken or poured cocktail, served in a tall slim-jim glass.

1/5 vodka, 4/5 orange juice. Shake together and pour over crushed ice. Gently pour galliano onto the top of the cocktail.

Alternatively, over the crushed ice pour vodka, orange juice, and galliano in the proportions given above.

**Highballs**   A poured cocktail, served in a highball glass.

About 1½ oz of spirit in a tall glass with an ice-cube, topped up with dry ginger ale *or* soda-water. Decorate with lemon rind.

The best known Highball is the *Horse's Neck*. This is made with brandy as the spirit, a few drops of angostura bitters, and a long spiral of lemon peel to decorate the glass.

**Kir**    A poured cocktail, served in a goblet wine glass.

Dry white burgundy wine (4 oz), cassis added to individual taste.

**Manhattan**    A stirred cocktail, served in a small cocktail glass.

2/3 rye whisky, 1/3 sweet vermouth, angostura bitters. Add a cherry.

**Martini Cocktail**    A stirred cocktail, served in a small cocktail glass.

2/3 dry gin, 1/3 dry vermouth, and squeezed lemon peel or an olive.

**Old Fashioned**    A poured cocktail, served in an old fashioned tumbler.

Angostura bitters on a sugar lump, bourbon or rye whisky, twist of lemon rind, cocktail cherry. (Many bars serve Scotch whisky this way.)

**Pimms** (No. 1 Cup)    This is a proprietary mixture which is mixed with lemonade and decorated with lemon, borage, cucumber, etc. in a tall glass. Its recipe is secret but it is based on gin.

**Pink Gin**    A few drops of angostura bitters is placed in a wine goblet which is then twirled so that the glass becomes pink. A jigger of Plymouth gin is then poured into the goblet with one ice-cube.

**Pink Lady**    A shaken cocktail, served in a double-sized cocktail glass.

1/2 white of one egg, gin, grenadine. Shake well to froth.

**Pousse Café**    Built in the glass in layers according to the specific gravity.

1) Grenadine 2) Crème de menthe 3) Parfait Amour 4) Tia Maria 5) Blue Curaçao 6) Benedictine 7) Brandy. Any other liqueurs may be used.

**Screwdriver**    A shaken cocktail, served in a double-sized cocktail glass.

1/3 vodka, 2/3 fresh orange juice, slice of orange. Add an ice-cube.

**Sidecar**    A shaken cocktail, served in a small cocktail glass.

1/2 brandy, 1/4 cointreau, 1/4 lemon juice.

**Sours**    contain lemon juice, egg-white, sugar and spirit, well shaken and served in a goblet or flute.

**Egg-Sour**    A shaken cocktail, served in a goblet wine glass.

Whole egg, juice of half a lemon, barspoon of sugar, orange curaçao, and brandy. Shaken well to form good froth. Pour with up and down moves.

**Tequila Sunrise**    A poured cocktail, in a tall slim-jim glass.

1/5 tequila, 4/5 orange juice. Pour the tequila and then the orange juice over crushed ice in the tall glass. Pour a small amount of grenadine on top. This will sink and give a sunrise effect. Add a half slice of orange.

**Pina Colada**    A shaken *or* poured cocktail, served in a double cocktail glass.

1/4 white rum, 1/2 pineapple juice, 1/4 coconut cream (or Malibu).

Shake, blend, or pour the ingredients and add a pineapple wedge.

**White Lady**    A shaken cocktail, served in a small cocktail glass.

Dry gin, cointreau, and lemon juice in equal quantities. Decorate with a cocktail cherry.

# Non-alcoholic Cocktails

**Cinderella**    1/3 orange juice, 1/3 lemon juice, 1/3 pineapple juice.

Shake and strain into a medium-sized wine glass or small tumbler.

**Parson's Special**    Glass of orange juice, yolk of one egg, grenadine (two dashes).

Shake and strain into a large glass and top up with soda-water.

**Pussyfoot**  1/3 fresh orange juice, 1/3 lemon juice. 1/3 lime juice, yolk of egg, dash of grenadine.

Shake well and serve in a medium wine glass.

# Cocktail Equipment

The equipment in a cocktail bar will normally consist of the following as minimum requirement:

Cocktail shakers; mixing glasses; bitters bottles; hawthorn strainer; muddler spoon; ice container, ice-maker, and ice-crusher; refrigerator; fruit knife and cutting board; corkscrew, crown cork opener; sugar basins for lump and caster sugar; small jugs for lemon juice, fresh cream, egg whites, etc.; glass-cloths and linen napkins; glassware in a variety of shapes and sizes; wine coolers; drinking straws; and a supply of decorative items such as miniature umbrellas, cocktail swords, pink elephants, mermaids, etc. An electric blender enables the bar-person to extend the range and scope of cocktails offered. No bar should be without Worcestershire sauce, and an adequate supply of fresh fruit, eggs, cream, milk, mint, olives, cucumber, pearl onions and cloves. Nutmeg and salt may also be required for certain drinks.

A **muddler spoon** is used to stir cocktails in the mixing glass. It may also be used for 'muddling', which is the old term for crushing sugar lumps or mint in the mixing glass using the flat, round end of the spoon. A well-prepared cocktail bartender will have placed a clean linen napkin on the bar top where he intends to work so that after stirring a cocktail the wet spoon may be placed down on the cloth. When the cloth becomes soiled it should be exchanged.

**Glassware** should *sparkle* and any spare minutes in the bar should be spent in re-polishing glasses. Well-positioned lighting can be used to show off glassware most attractively. The *shape* of glassware used for particular cocktails is of very minor importance, but the *size* of the glass matters a great deal.

An expert and well-trained bartender will not usually need to measure any of the ingredients in a cocktail. His experience and continual practice will be sufficient to give fine and accurate judgement of the precise amount of each subtle flavour needed to complete the cocktail, so that no one taste overshadows the rest. That is the essential magic of cocktail expertise.

# Part 7:

# Cellar-work

*Cellar Equipment*
*Cellar Routines*
*Beer Containers*

# Cellar Equipment

Beer and wine cellars must be uncluttered places. The most important space-fillers in this cool area must be the main saleable commodity. Casks in use (on ullage) will be supported on *stillions* (called *thrawls* in some parts of the north of Britain). A stillion, or stillaging, is the wooden rack or brick platform upon which the casks are placed for service. *Keg* pressurised beer containers are usually situated together in one area of the cellar along with the necessary $CO_2$ *gas cylinders* strapped or bracketed to the wall. Make sure that gas cylinders are not used without a *reducing valve* in position on top of the cylinder. Correct cylinder procedures prevent accidents.

*Gas cylinder and reducing valve*

*Beer engines* are not really engines in the usual sense, but pumps pulled by hand using a handle in the bar. They must be cleaned weekly when the *pipe-lines* are cleaned, and must be stripped down and inspected on a monthly basis. New washers may be needed etc. Some engines work by *carbon dioxide top pressure*, which applies force downwards on to the beer in the cask and drives a measured amount up into the bar when a button is pressed.

*Electrical impeller pumps* situated in the cellar can be installed to dispense an accurate amount of beer into the glass in the bar, again when the bartender presses a button. They should not be installed in cellars which are liable to flood.

*Pipe cleaning bottles* are used to clean pressurised container pipelines. With the gas turned off, the assembly head should be taken from the keg and locked onto the two-gallon cleaning bottle containing cleaning fluid. The $CO_2$ should be turned on and the pipes filled with the fluid. After about one hour the process should be repeated using clean water. Automatic beerline cleaning equipment, as shown here, is also popular now; being fully automated it leaves the cellar-man free to do other equally important tasks.

*Pipe-cleaning*

Small equipment should be kept free from dust and insects, preferably in a lidded box. *Taps* may be of brass or stainless steel and should be sterilised after use by plunging them into very hot water. Do not leave taps in hot water for more than one hour. Plastic taps are now being recommended by some major brewers.

*Dip-sticks* are used to determine how much beer is left in a cask. The dip-stick is placed into the cask through the *shive*, when withdrawn it indicates how much beer remains unsold. *Scotches* are triangular blocks of wood which are used to prevent a beer cask from rolling from side to side.

*Shives* are round pieces of hard wood which are placed in the bung-hole of the beer cask just before it is sent out from the brewery after *racking* (filling). The shive has a small hole in the centre which does not go completely through the wood. When the cask is vented, the hole is completed by punching out the thin centre section with a *wooden mallet*. The hole will permit gas to escape from the cask. *Spiles* are used in the hole to allow or prevent the $CO_2$ gas from escaping. They are small pegs made of two different types of wood. The *hardwood* spile, when placed in the shive, does not allow any gas to escape. Instead, pressure builds up in the cask and the beer regains its condition (frothy

*Tap, shive, keystone bush and spiles*

head). The softer spile is made of *bamboo* and, when placed in the shive, it allows the gas to escape and so prevents the beer from being too gassy and difficult to serve.

*Filters* must only be used in the cellar to return sound beer to a cask. For instance, beer which has been drawn out of the pipes before pipe-cleaning started. Filters must be kept clean and used with clean filter papers.

*Hoists* are used in a few large hotels to deliver liquor stocks of wines, spirits, beers and minerals upstairs. They do present a safety hazard and staff must be well drilled in their use.

## Disposal of bottles

The method of disposal of bottles depends upon the amount of space available in the bar. *Empty crates* may be used but they have to be carried out of the way as soon as they are full, and handling dirty crates means dirty hands. *Skips* on wheels are very hygienic, and are simply and easily pushed out of the bar when full. They are now made of glass fibre. *Wicker baskets*, with wheels and a metal insert to catch the drips, are still found in some public bars.

*Chutes* may be built into bar counters. Bottles placed in the chute travel down a tube to the cellar below. They are good so long as they are not blocked by bottles which are too wide, e.g. Benedictine bottles.

*Behind the bar*

# Cellar Routines

The cellar-man's role is similar to that of the stage-manager in a theatre, he is rarely seen but if his work is not up to standard then the results will show up in the box-office takings! Customers will not drink in his house if the beer is not in good condition. The conditions of work are not ideal and whilst his clerical work may be above ground, much of his day-to-day activity will be in cool, often damp, cellars.

The ideal cellar is located in the basement of the building at a constant temperature of around 58°F (14°C). It should be immediately below the bar to avoid too long a pipe-line between the cask and the beer engine. If the cellar is below drainage level a pump will have been installed to ensure dry conditions.

The floor of the cellar should be of hard granolithic material with a slight downward slope to a tiled centre channel covered by metal gridding. The corners where the floor meets the walls should be rounded to prevent the accumulation of dirt and the encouragement of insect pests.

Because of condensation the walls must not be tiled and whitewashed common brick is most usual in British cellars. Some have the last half-metre or so faced with bitumen as a damp-seal. A sink with cold water is essential in a beer cellar. Hot water is an advantage but, if available, the hot water supply must be brought through the wall directly where it is required, to prevent raising the cellar temperature and spoiling the beer.

The ceiling should be about three metres high and insulated. It should be whitewashed regularly. Any suspended electric light bulb should be protected by a detachable wire mesh.

The delivery ramp area can become slimy and hazardous in bad weather. It can also become dirty quickly, with dust and leaves blown in at delivery times. Great care should be taken to keep the ramp clean, with the steps washed down and the side walls whitewashed. The licensee has a duty to the public to keep the walk-over flaps and ramp in a good state of repair.

Ventilation should be adequate to ensure that, when a pint of draught beer is pulled from the cask, it is replaced with the same volume of clean air which is sucked into the cask via the shive. Smells must be avoided in the cellar as they will cause the beer to deteriorate. Carbolic soaps, disinfectants, oils, channel blocks, dead mice or birds (or the family cat misbehaving in the cellar!), will all have a disastrous effect upon the beer.

Heating is not usually required in a beer cellar but in a prolonged spell of ice and snow, with very low temperatures, it may be necessary to provide some gentle heat. This may be best achieved by placing two ordinary house bricks in front of, and quite close to, a small portable gas or electric fire. To cool the cellar, wet sacks placed near an open door, or even over the beer casks, will quickly bring the temperature down.

Small equipment—taps, spiles, corks, etc.—should be stored in a clean cupboard or a lidded box, or in a 'cellar tidy' bag.

All beer pipe-lines should be cleaned weekly with a diluted pipe-clean fluid, and the cellar floor washed down weekly with a weak solution of *chloride of lime* (mild bleach). These essential jobs are best attended to on the days when you are least busy with deliveries.

Casks will be properly settled if they are tapped 24 hours before they are needed, so the cellar-man needs to anticipate and estimate the following day's requirement.

*Tapping a cask*

Re-ordering should be carried out on one set day every week after checking the bottle stocks of beers, wines, minerals, etc. Strict rotation of stocks must be exercised, with new crates placed at the rear and old stock pulled to the front for first issue.

To filter beer is not in itself illegal, but to return to cask any over-spill or 'slops' is an offence. And to mix or dilute beer in the cask, or to adulterate any product for sale, is a serious illegal act.

It is not necessary to throw away the first pint of beer drawn from each pump at the start of the serving session. Modern dispense equipment ensures a sound pint from the first pull.

## Cloudy beer

Beer may be cloudy if the cask has been disturbed, if the pipe-lines are unclean or if the cellar temperature is too low. If the cellar-man has forgotten to remove the spile from the shive of a cask of draught beer before the bar-person tries to pull a pint, the result will probably be cloudy beer in the cask and no beer in the glass, as it is not possible to pull beer with the spile in position.

### Sour beer

Sour beer may be caused by adding stale beer to a good cask, or if the cask has been on service too long, or if there are strong odours in the cellar. Heavy yeast deposits in pipes and equipment can also cause the beer to turn sour. Many licensees believe that a heavy thunderstorm can seriously damage the beer.

### Flat beer

Flat beer may be due to faulty spile control, i.e. having a soft spile in position when a hard one is needed to build up pressure. Grease from pies or sandwiches left on the rim of the glass by the customer's mouth can make the next pint appear flat. Detergent on glasses also makes beer lose its head and a cellar temperature which is too low will have the same effect.

# Beer Containers

### Casks

The sizes of beer casks in use in Britain are as follows:
    *Hoghead* holds approximately 54 gallons (432 pints)
    *Barrel* holds approximately 36 gallons (288 pints)
    *Kilderkin* holds approximately 18 gallons (144 pints)
    *Firkin* holds approximately 9 gallons (72 pints)
    *Pin* holds approximately $4\frac{1}{2}$ gallons (36 pints)
The casks were originally shaped by *coopers*, from *oak* staves bound by metal bands. Most modern casks are of metal but are handled in the same way as wood. Casks are placed on the *stillion* in a horizontal position and are naturally conditioned. This means that the contents give off their own gas ($CO_2$), which forms the head or froth that is welcomed on the pint in the bar.

*Beer casks*

Beer casks should have a cork placed in the keystone plug as soon as the tap is removed. A *spile* should be driven into the *shive* with a wooden mallet. The container will then be protected against insects, airborne bacteria and mould. Beer casks are steam-cleaned at the brewery before *racking* (filling) as casks which have been contaminated can cause the beer to go out of condition. Sulphur tapers are burned in casks which are still suspect after steam cleaning. This method has been used since Roman times.

## Kegs

Kegs are metal containers of beer which are used in a vertical position in the cellar. The condition of keg beer is provided by cylinders of $CO_2$ gas which are strapped or bracketed to the wall near to the keg. The sizes of keg in use in British bars are usually five gallons and ten gallons. It is strongly recommended that kegs should be finished within four days of delivery, if possible, to maintain the very best condition. Kegs of Guinness do not require a gas cylinder as the gas is actually contained in the top of the keg.

*Beer kegs*

### Bottles

Beer bottles are usually brown in colour. This is to protect the contents from sunlight, which is known to be harmful to beer. A few well-known brewers produce beer which is sold in clear bottles, but strict instructions are given to ensure that sunlight is avoided. It is assumed that the beer will be sold and consumed before the effects of prolonged sunlight have interfered with the product.

Bottled beers are sold in plastic crates which are light to handle and stack conveniently and safely. *Small* bottles are of not less than a half-pint and are crated in two dozens. They are capped with crown corks made of metal and lined with cork. *Large* bottles are of not less than one pint and are delivered in crates containing one dozen. Most pint bottles have crown corks but some breweries prefer the screw stoppers. *Flagons* hold two pints and are crated in half-dozens.

Disposable plastic bottles containing one litre, which are used for mineral waters, have not been generally introduced for beer sales to commercial establishments, although one brewery now uses disposable bottles of lightweight glass. *Nips* are the smallest bottles containing one-third of a pint. The beer sold in nips is stronger than most other beers and is referred to as a *baby*!

Deposits are paid on glass bottles when the customer buys the beer in the off-licence or public house off-sales. Special care must be taken to control the empties, as a considerable amount of money can be lost by inefficient security of empties.

### Cans

Seven-pint cans can be purchased for party use, as well as one-pint and half-pint sizes of a variety of beers and lagers.

### Tank beer

The most modern system of beer storage in public house cellars is the bulk tank delivery. The beer is delivered by road tankers to the licensed premises where the beer is piped into the cellar and directed into large tanks, which are usually of ninety gallons (equal to two-and-a-half barrels) and 180 gallons (equal to five barrels).

*Beer tanks*

*The Campaign for Real Ale* is an organisation which was originally set up in St. Albans by a group of beer drinkers. Its aims are to encourage the brewing, conditioning, and serving of beers in the traditional way. There are now branches in many parts of the UK and a quarterly newspaper is produced. CAMRA have now entered the property business and own public houses.

# Part 8:

# Brewing and Distilling

*Commodities Used in Brewing Beer*
*Brewing*
*Cider and Perry*
*Mixers and Minerals*
*Distillation*
*Gin*
*Cognac*
*Rum*
*Scotch*
*Whiskey*
*Calvados*
*Other Spirits*
*Speciality Coffees*
*Liqueurs*
*Herb Liqueurs*

# Commodities Used in Brewing Beer

## Liquor

This is the name used in the brewery for water. It includes all the water which is used, including the washing and cleaning as well as the brewing itself. It must be abundant and pure. The finest water for beer-making is found at *Burton-upon-Trent*, where the *hard* water is used in the manufacture of pale ales and bitter, and from the deep artesian wells under *London*, where the *soft* water is important in the production of mild ales, brown ales, and stout. It is estimated that each brewery uses seven times as much liquor as the beer produced.

## Malt

Malt is made from *barley*, which is produced in many parts of Britain but mainly in Norfolk, Yorkshire, Suffolk, and Hampshire. The barley is harvested and quickly dried out on the perforated floor of the *kiln*, to prevent mould forming before storage. When it is needed, the barley grains are *steeped* (soaked) in water for about three days. The damp barley is laid on the malting shed floor about 10 cm deep. The conditions are just right in the malting shed for germination to take place.

*The barley harvest*

Warmth, moisture and oxygen are all necessary to enable the shoot and rootlets to form: the grain is damp from its soaking; the floor or the malting shed provides the warmth; and the grain is turned daily with wooden shovels to provide the oxygen. Modern maltings are entirely mechanical, but the results are the same. The *enzyme cytase* breaks down the cell walls which enclose the granules of starch and the *enzyme diastase* converts the insoluble starch into fermentable soluble sugar.

When the grain has been turned for between five and ten days the *maltster* decides whether he needs pale malts for light ales or roasted malts for dark beers or stouts. The germination is stopped by raising the temperature to dry out the moisture. If dark malts are required, then intense heat is applied, which turns the grain darker in colour and will contribute most of the final colour to the beer. The final correction of the colour is made by adding caramel. Malted barley will keep in good condition for several years, if necessary, after the malting process.

## Sugars

*Invert sugar* is the most usual sugar used in brewing, as it is the easiest to ferment. It is added when the wort (see page 121) is boiled in the copper, with less sugar added for the bitter beers and light ales. Sweeter beers, like brown ales and sweet stouts, also have sugar added to them in the form of *primings* just before they leave the brewery.

## Hops

Hops are a member of the nettle (hemp) family and are produced in September in hop gardens in Kent, Hereford and Worcester, and Hampshire. They are grown on *binds* (strings) more than three metres high. The female flowers are used as they contain a bitter dust called *lupalin* which contains tannins and resins. The plants cling their way up the binds in a clockwise direction (the opposite of runner beans). They are harvested by machines and the flower cones are dried in *oast-houses* and packed in large 1½ cwt sacks called *pockets*. The reasons for adding hops to the brew are three-fold: *flavouring*—giving beer its bitter taste; *cleansing*—the hot liquid passes through the spent hops in the hop-back after boiling in the copper, which removes much of the sediment

*Hops*

and solids from the wort; and *preserving*—beer will keep for longer in good condition when more hops are used, due to the presence of tannin which acts as a preservative.

The hops are removed before fermentation starts and the spent hops are sold to the farmers as fertiliser. Hop extracts in condensed form are now being used in some breweries as they require less storage space than large pockets.

## Yeast

Yeast is a fungus which reproduces itself by cell division, leaving the brewer with about five times more at the end of the process than at the beginning. The surplus is sold for such products as Yeastvite and Marmite etc. The yeast converts the sugars in the wort into alcohol and carbon dioxide gas. The two varieties used in brewing are: *Saccharomyces cerevisae*, which forms as a scum on *top* of fermenting *beer*; and *Saccharomyces carlsbergensis*, which is used in the production of *lager* and sinks to the *bottom* of the vessel during fermentation.

## Finings

Traditionally, this is the substance obtained from tropical fish bladders (isinglas), used to clarify beer by causing the sediment to sink and leaving the beer brilliant.

# Brewing

Beer is the result of the fermentation of the sweet liquid known as *wort*, which is obtained by soaking ground malted barley. When the malted barley arrives at the brewery in sacks, it is stored until it is required. Until recently breweries were always housed in very tall buildings, so that the movement of the liquids throughout the process would be by gravity and pumps would not be necessary. But some modern breweries have now been built in low horizontal buildings.

1. The brewing process starts in the *mill* where the malted barley is ground into *grist*.

2. The grist is fed into the mash-tun where it is *sparged* with boiling water sprayed from rotating arms.

3. As soon as all the sugar has been soaked out of the grist it is piped to the *copper*, where it is boiled with *hops* and *sugar* for between one-and-a-half and two hours. In modern breweries the 'copper' is made of stainless steel. The left-over solids from the mash-tun are sold as cattle-cake (farm feedstuffs).

4. After boiling, the hot wort is directed with the hops to the *hop-back*, which is a large tank with a perforated floor. The hot liquid passes through the spent hops, from which all the bitter flavour has been removed, leaving behind all the sediment and floating particles. The hops perform the function of a first *filter*. The finished hops are sold as hop fertiliser for garden and agricultural use.

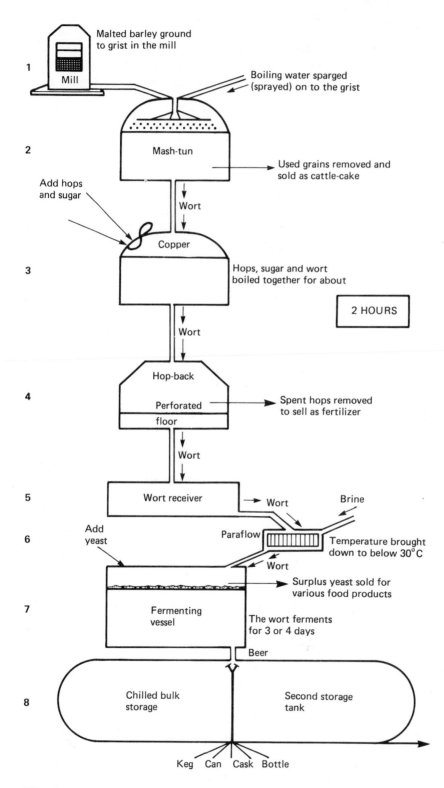

**1** Mill — Malted barley ground to grist in the mill

Boiling water sparged (sprayed) on to the grist

**2** Mash-tun — Used grains removed and sold as cattle-cake

Wort

Add hops and sugar

**3** Copper — Hops, sugar and wort boiled together for about

2 HOURS

Wort

**4** Hop-back
Perforated
floor — Spent hops removed to sell as fertilizer

Wort

**5** Wort receiver — Wort — Brine

**6** Add yeast — Paraflow — Temperature brought down to below 30°C

Wort

Surplus yeast sold for various food products

**7** Fermenting vessel — The wort ferments for 3 or 4 days

Beer

**8** Chilled bulk storage — Second storage tank

Keg   Can   Cask   Bottle

*The brewing process*

5. The liquid next passes into the *wort-receiver* where it can be held if not immediately required.

6. In order that the yeast can become active and fermentation take place, it is necessary to bring down the temperature. This is done in the *paraflow*, where the hot liquid circulates between stainless steel plates with cold water or brine flowing in the opposite direction on the other side of the plates. The temperature must come down to less than 30°C. Yeast can only operate between 5°C and 30°C.

7. The cooled wort continues into the fermenting vessel where *yeast* is *pitched* into it. Many brewers are still using the same culture of yeast from thirty years ago. This is because yeast reproduces itself more than fourfold, whilst consuming the sugar in the wort and converting it to alcohol and $CO_2$ gas. Some vessels are open to the air, while others are enclosed so that the gas can be collected for use in beer that is bottled, canned, and in kegs. The yeast on the surface of the brew looks like a scum, which gradually changes to take on a 'rocky' and later a 'cauliflower' appearance. The Customs and Excise officers are able to visit to test the specific gravity before fermentation starts, to determine the *duty* payable.

8. The beer passes into chilled bulk storage until required for *racking* into casks, or kegs, for bottling or canning, or transportation by tanker.

# Cider and Perry

Cider is known to have been drunk in Britain before the Romans came and the method of making it was perfected by the monks in the Middle Ages. Farmhouses in the south-west of England, and especially in Herefordshire, Gloucestershire, Worcestershire, Devonshire, Dorset and Somerset, have made cider for centuries. Records show that many farmers in these counties regularly paid their labourers up to one-fifth of their wages in cider!

Cider is made in England from mid-September to the end of November. Modern harvesting methods include machinery attached to the tractor which firmly grips the trunk of the apple tree and shakes the ripe fruit onto the ground. A large blower machine forces the apples into the wide open spaces between the rows of trees and the fruit is then picked up mechanically. At the cider mill the apples are carried by water from the silos to be tipped into the mill. Here they are milled to a pulp which is called the *cheese*. This is wrapped in coarse sack-cloth and pressed under a hydraulic press. After settling, the juice is pumped into fermenting vats where yeast is added to start the conversion into cider. The sugar will be converted to alcohol and $CO_2$ gas. The fermentation takes between four and twelve weeks. The cider is then allowed to mature for several weeks more before it is released for sale.

**Pomagne** is the most popular brand of sparkling cider, made by a process of secondary fermentation in the bottle, not unlike the champagne method.

*Picking apples for cider*

**Scrumpy** is the popular name for rough homemade and strong farmhouse cider.

**Draught cider** is made when a small amount of sugar and yeast is added to each cask before it leaves the mill to ensure a natural sparkle or condition.

More than sixty million gallons of cider is drunk annually in the UK. Some cider is sold as still cider while other brands are carbonated with carbon dioxide gas after chilling and filtering.

## Perry

Perry is made from pears, using the same techniques as for cider making.

124

# Mixers and Minerals

## Artificial mineral waters

These are made up of six ingredients:
1) Pure filtered water
2) Sugar or other permitted sweeteners
3) Fruit juice or concentrated essences of fruits
4) Citric or tartaric acid to stimulate the appetite
5) Flavourings
6) Carbon dioxide gas for sparkling effervescence

It is estimated that in the UK we each consume eight gallons of soft drinks every year.

*Joseph Priestly* succeeded in making the first sparkling mineral water artificially in 1772. It had long been known that the sparkling spring water found at the 'spas' was beneficial to health. The Admiralty were persuaded by Priestly that the blood disease 'scurvy', which was caused by lack of fresh vegetables or drinking water, could be cured by carbonated water flavoured with lime-juice. From this drink the British sailors soon came to be known as 'limeys'.

*Mixers*, such as bitter lemon, ginger ale, soda-water, lemonade etc., show an excellent profit margin and the good salesperson will encourage the customer to use them instead of just water in a glass of spirit. An attractive display of minerals and mixers in a bar, along with appropriate sales promotion material, help to achieve what is known as the 'silent selling' technique. Shandy, Zing, Coca-cola, 7-up, Pepsi-cola, Vimto, Tizer, and ginger beer, along with numerous others, join with squashes, cordials and syrups to complicate the drinker's choice. Very popular with slimmers are the low-calorie slim-line editions of the minerals. Fruit juices, especially tomato, orange, grapefruit, and pineapple have become very popular with drivers since stricter drink/driving legislation was introduced.

## Natural mineral waters

These are forced from the ground already naturally impregnated with mineral elements; in some cases, carbonic acid gas ($CO_2$) in solution makes them sparkle. Many of the waters are considered to have curative powers. In Victorian times many patients were advised to travel to the spa towns to take the waters.

The names on the labels denote the place of origin. More than 70 per cent of the waters sold in Britain come from *France*. Of these, *Perrier*, from the south and *Vichy Celestins*, from the Massif Central, are the most popular sparkling waters, while *Evian* from Savoie is the market leader in still waters. *San Pellegrino* comes from near Milan in *Italy* and is sparkling. West *Germany*'s best spring water is *Apollinaris*, which is naturally sparkling. *Malvern* water is the most famous still mineral water from *Great Britain*, produced by Schweppes at Colwall Springs in Herefordshire, while *Ashbourne* in Derbyshire produces the finest sparkling mineral water in the UK.

# Distillation

The first spirits were made more than 4 000 years ago. Opinion is divided as to whether the first stills were used by the Chinese to make perfumes, or by the Arabs to make potable (drinkable) alcohol. The stills are known by the word *alambic*, which is of Arabic origin.

Because ethyl alcohol vapourises (boils) at a lower temperature (78°C) than water, it is possible to separate the alcohol from the water. There are two principal methods of making potable alcohol. These are the *pot still*, used world-wide over centuries, and the 'factory' process, which was invented in 1831 by Aeneas Coffey. This is usually known as the *patent* or *continuous* still and is capable of producing large amounts of highly rectified (very pure) spirit in a very short time. Whichever method is used, the result will be *colourless*. Any colour in the final spirit comes mainly from the wood of the casks in which it is matured, or artificially from caramel.

## The pot still

1. Needs cleaning out after every boiling.
2. Requires constant attention to maintain the required temperature. (If the heat rises to the boiling point of water, steam would go over with the alcoholic vapour and there would be no separation of alcohol.)

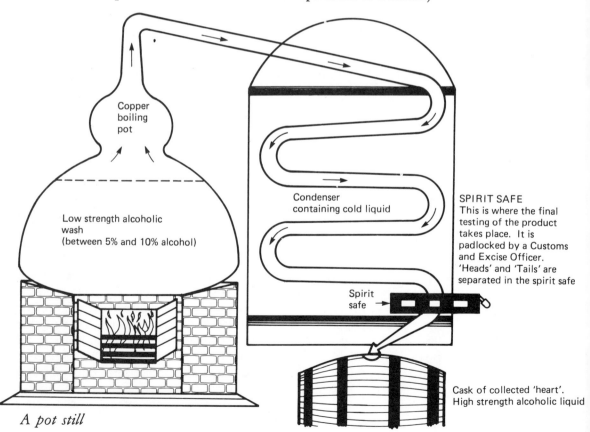

Copper boiling pot

Low strength alcoholic wash (between 5% and 10% alcohol)

Condenser containing cold liquid

SPIRIT SAFE
This is where the final testing of the product takes place. It is padlocked by a Customs and Excise Officer. 'Heads' and 'Tails' are separated in the spirit safe

Spirit safe

Cask of collected 'heart'. High strength alcoholic liquid

*A pot still*

3. Spirits made by this method contain impurities. These are the full heavy flavours which would be removed if distillation was fierce. (Pot still distillation is gentle.)

4. As many of these impurities take time to mature, and can be harmful in the early months, distillers are legally bound to mature pot still spirits for a minimum of two years before sale.

5. Distillation will need to be carried out twice in order to reach the point of acceptable drinkable alcohol.

6. Maturing will take place at high strength 70° OIML (123° Sikes). This will be let down to drinking strength 40° OIML (70° Sikes) with pure water before bottling.

7. Evaporation usually takes place during maturation (3 per cent p.a.).

*Heads* (or foreshots): These are the toxic methyl alcohols (methylated spirits) which come off first in the process. These must be removed.
*Heart:* Sound drinkable alcohol.
*Tails:* (or feints): The poor quality, low strength, last part which is usually put back into the next pot for re-boiling.

*Spirits made by the pot-still method* include: malt whisky, Irish whiskey, brandy, pungent rums and Geneva gins.

*Note* Spirits improve in wood but never in bottle.

## The patent still

This is the most modern way of producing spirit for use in chemical plants and laboratories, as well as for perfumes, petroleum products, and alcohol for social drinking.

The patent still was invented in Dublin in 1830 by Aeneas Coffey, who was a Customs and Excise officer. Its main characteristics are:

1. It needs only one operation to produce a drinkable product.

2. It does not need cleaning out after every boiling.

3. It produces a much stronger spirit than the pot still.

4. Nearly all impurities are removed to give a very pure spirit.

5. Products do not need to be matured before sale. (Patent still spirits may be sold as soon as produced.)

6. Heads and tails are automatically removed in the process.

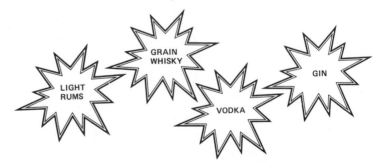

The low-strength alcoholic 'wash' which is used in distillation could be:
*Wine* which when distilled would become *brandy*.
*Beer* which when distilled could become *whisky*, *vodka*, or *gin*.
*Cider* which when distilled in Normandy becomes *calvados*.

Great care should be taken to avoid illegally distilled spirits, as these probably contain toxic methyl alcohols which may not have been removed during distillation. Consumption of methyl alcohol, even in small quantities, is dangerous and over a fairly short time will cause serious damage to the brain and nervous system.

---

Any commodity containing starch or sugar can be fermented to give low strength alcohol. It is possible therefore to distil a drinkable spirit from any commodity which has fermented with yeast.

A distiller's licence is required to produce high strength alcohol.

---

## The apparatus used to produce patent still spirits

The apparatus takes the form of two large columns as shown below. Each column is more than fifteen metres tall, often as high as a three-storey building. The rate of production of highly rectified (very pure) spirit can be as high as 10,000 gallons in one hour.

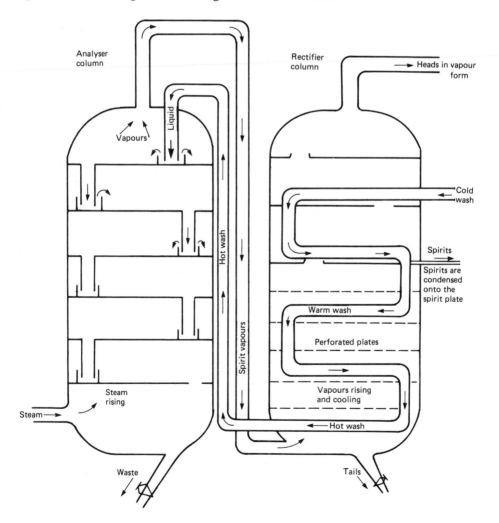

# Gin

## Origins

Gin is diluted alcohol which has been distilled in a *patent still* and afterwards carefully flavoured with plant extracts, known as *botanicals*, and re-distilled in a pot still. It was first made in 1577 by *Sylvius Van Leyden*, a *Dutch* chemistry professor, who sold it as a medicine. It had long been established that oil of juniper was effective in the treatment of kidney trouble and gout. *Genièvre* is French for *juniper* and the name of gin is taken from the first part of the word. *Geneva* is the Dutch translation of *juniper*, and has no connection with the town or lake in Switzerland.

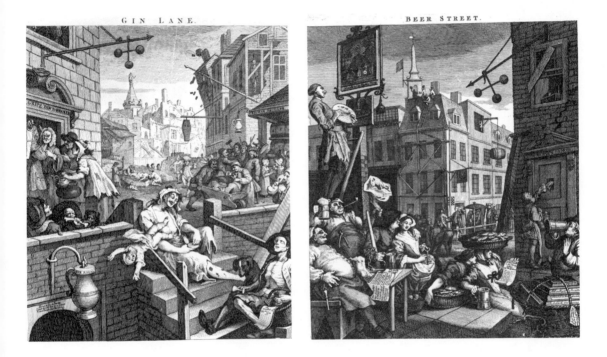

Gin was described as 'Dutch Courage' by the soldiers who fought in the Low Countries, when they returned to England with *William of Orange* in 1688. From that time gin became very popular in England, especially among the working-class population. It was sold by chemists, grocers, tobacconists, barbers, market traders, and even on street corners. The consumption of gin increased so rapidly that it became a social evil. In 1729 one house in every four in London was distilling gin, made in illicit stills from dregs of beer or even from rotting vegetables. 'Mother's ruin' caused much mental illness, and alcoholism was widespread. Some employers even made part-payment of wages in gin! The *Temperance* movement was born out of this social degradation. *Hogarth's* famous etchings (shown above) sought to point out that *beer* was healthier than *gin*.

The Nonconformist religious movements, government taxes, licences for distilling, and the growth in industrial prosperity all contributed to the gradual control of the gin menace. Taverns became more respectable and, in place of rough inns with straw on the floor, the Victorians built brassy 'gin palaces'. Gone were the riots and drunkeness of the late 1730s. Gin was at last accepted into middle-class drawing-rooms.

From 1880, cocktails and mixed drinks became popular in the USA. Gin proved to be one of the most suitable ingredients because of its colour. During the years of 'Prohibition', when alcohol was forbidden in North America (1919 to 1935), the illicit trading in poor quality 'bath-tub gin' once more reached a peak.

## Types of gin

*London dry gin*   This gin may be made anywhere in the world and is the most common. It is unsweetened. Booths, Gordons, Squires, Burroughs, Seagers, and Seagrams are all well-known manufacturers.

*Plymouth gin*   More pungent than London dry, it is produced by Coates in Devonshire. Plymouth Gin and angostura bitters should be used in 'pink gin'.

*Fruit gins*   These are flavoured gins which may be made from any fruit, the most usual being *oranges*, *lemons*, or *sloes*. This last, made from the fruit of the blackthorn bush, involves steeping the bruised sloes in London dry gin. Sloe gin may be sweetened.

*Geneva gin*   Geneva Gin is made in Holland entirely by the pot still method. Bols and De Kuyper are the best-known manufacturers of this gin, which is popularly known as 'Hollands'.

*Malt wine*   Malt wine is a type of gin made in the Netherlands by *four* distillations in a pot still.

*Old Tom*   Sweet gin made in Scotland mainly for export. It is gin sweetened with sugar-syrup and was originally used in a 'Tom Collins' cocktail.

*Cold compounded gins*   These are made from cheap neutral spirit flavoured with essences.

## Production

The base product used for gin in the UK is *maize*, but it is possible and permissable to make the spirit from any fermentable foodstuff. The Dutch gins, Geneva and malt wine are usually made from *rye*. Malted barley is also sometimes used in gin manufacture.

Because most gin is highly rectified in a patent still, all the impurities have been removed. This means that it can be sold as soon as it is produced. The pure spirit is reduced with distilled water and steeped with *botanicals* before re-distillation in a *pot still*. The list of botanicals used by each company is a closely guarded secret, but they all feature *juniper berries* and *coriander seeds*. The spirit is then let down with pure water to 70° Sikes (40 per cent alcohol) before bottling.

# Cognac

Brandy may be made anywhere in the world but cognac can only be made in a limited area of France called the Charente and the Charente Maritime. To brand something is to burn it and 'Brandywyn' was first burned or distilled nearly 500 years ago in order to transport it on ships. The idea was to add about nine times its volume of water to change it back to the original wine when it reached its destination, as one cask of brandy took up much less space than ten casks of wine. But the original flavour was impossible to recover.

The commercial production of cognac was pioneered by British developers, *Martell* from the Channel Isles, *Hine* from Dorset, and *Hennessy* from Ireland.

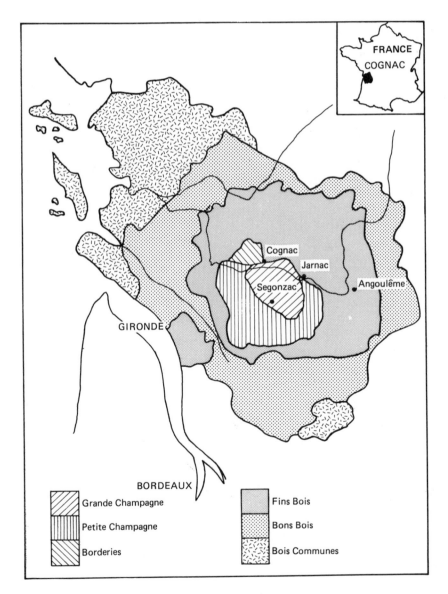

FRANCE
COGNAC

Cognac
Jarnac
Segonzac
Angoulême
GIRONDE
BORDEAUX

Grande Champagne
Petite Champagne
Borderies
Fins Bois
Bons Bois
Bois Communes

Cognac is an AOC spirit and by Appellation Contrôlée rules must be made in a pot still in the district of the Charente river.

The grapes from which cognac is made are mainly the *St. Emilion*, the *Folle Blanche*, and the *Colombard*, and the wine they produce is very low in alcohol. After distillation, the cognac is colourless and receives its colour from the fine casks of *Limousin oak* from the forests of Limoges, 145 miles east of Cognac. This wood is rich in *tannin* and is ideal for the maturing of fine brandy. The soil in the centre of the region is *chalk* and vines dominate the landscape, but towards the lower quality parts of Cognac the chalk starts to give way to heavier clay, and woodlands outnumber the vineyards.

The *stars* on the labels of brandy have little significance these days but originally indicated the number of years of maturation. *VSOP* means *Very Special Old Pale* and, along with XO of Hennessy, denotes that the cognac is older than other cognacs, although it is only the same alcoholic strength. Brandy sold in the UK must be a minimum of three years old before sale. French law dictates that VSOP must be four years old before export. It is good practice to serve these older matured cognacs at the customer's table in the restaurant.

'Fine champagne' is the finest cognac, blended from the two best districts—Grande Champagne (more than 50 per cent) and Petite Champagne.

*Brouillis:* The result of the first distillation of cognac.
*La Bonne Chauffe:* The drinkable 'Heart' of the second distillation.
*Note* Like other spirits brandy does *not* improve in bottle.

*A brandy balloon*

## Other brandies

*Armagnac*   Also AOC a fine quality earthy brandy from France.
*Asbach*   Fine quality 'Weinbrand' (German).
*Eau de Vie de Marc*   French made from the pips and stalks of grapes (inexpensive).
*Grappa*   Similar, from Italy.

# Rum

### The liquid gold of the Caribbean

'A spirit distilled from sugar-cane products in sugar-cane-growing countries.' (Definition of 1909 Royal Commission on Potable Spirits.) 'Saccharum' is the Latin name for sweetness.

Many of the rum-producing areas of the Caribbean are former British colonial territories. Many of the sugar plantations where rum was born were fired and cut by slaves who had been brought to the Caribbean from their native Africa by British sailing vessels. A crude form of rum was made on the sugar estates by the slaves, even after a hard day's work. The Devonshire sailors' name for it was 'Rumbullion'. A rough liquor distilled in small pot stills, and drunk without maturing, rumbullion meant 'kill devil'.

In the manufacture of rum today, the most usual method is to make up a wash which is obtained from fermented molasses left over from the sugar-refining process. The alternative is to crush the sweet sugar-cane between rollers into 'bagasse', which is then fermented with yeast to give the *wash* ready for distillation.

Some well-known rums are made in a pot still. These have full heavy flavours and a pungent 'nose'. Jamaican rums, such as Lemon Hart, are very popular in cold northern climates. Countries that are too cold to produce their own sugar-cane often buy quantities of these pungent rums to blend with their own spirit, often made from sugar-beet. The resulting blend will be labelled 'imitation rum'. The most famous example is the German *Rum Verschnitt* (verschnitt means 'imitation').

Lighter rums are made by the patent still method. They have less flavour and some of the best examples are the rums of Barbados and Trinidad, both of which are used in the UK for blending.

Guyana is famous for rums which are a blend of full-flavoured pot-

*The Caribbean*

*Slaves being fettered and taken on board a slave ship*

still products and lighter patent-still rums. *Captain Morgan* and *Lamb's Navy* are typical, each containing approximately one-third from the pot stills.

White rum is increasing in popularity, especially since the drinking of cocktails has regained popularity, as it provides the character and flavour of rum without affecting the colour of the cocktail. The *Bacardi* family, producers of white rum, moved out of Cuba in 1959—just before the revolution when *Fidel Castro* took over. They took with them the technical expertise and the secrets of the Bacardi process of re-flavouring. Bacardi is now being distilled in the Bahamas, Puerto Rico, Mexico, Brazil, Miami in the USA, Bermuda, Martinique, Canada, and Venezuela. Other white rums include *Tropicana*, *Dry Cane*, *Daiquiri*, and *White Diamond*.

Owing to the hot sunshine of the Caribbean area and the rate of evaporation of rum during its maturation period, which could be as high as 50 per cent per annum, most of the rum is brought to *Scotland* to mature in the cellars of *United Rum Merchants* at *Dundee*. Here the climate ensures an evaporation rate of no more than 3 per cent per year. The strength of spirit during the maturation period of three years is very much higher than the strength at the point of sale. Maturing strength is between 130° Sikes (74 per cent) and 145° Sikes (83 per cent). After a minimum of three years the rum is 'let down' to drinking strength of

70 Sikes (40 per cent) with natural soft or distilled water. Recent legislation lays down that rum may now be sold as soon as it is produced.

The colour of dark rum comes from *caramel*, itself a product of sugar processes.

**Puncheon**   This is a wooden cask holding 110 gallons.
**Grog**   This was the mixture of rum and water which was issued daily to the British navy between 1740 and 1970. Admiral Vernon, known as 'Old Grog' because of his coarse cloth cloak, attempted to stamp out drunkenness by issuing two quarter-pints of neat rum diluted with water, to every sailor, with six hours between issues. This tradition was discontinued in 1970 because the Admiralty thought it was no longer in keeping with a modern navy!

# Scotch

*Scotch* is the name given to whisky distilled in Scotland. Proprietary scotch sold all over the world, under hundreds of different labels, is a *blend* of:

*Grain* whisky distilled in a *patent* still from *maize*.
and
*Malt* whisky distilled in a *pot* still from malted *barley*.
Such blending began in 1860 and the resulting product has proved far more acceptable to the Englishman's taste than the malt whiskies before that time.

*Deluxe whiskies*, which are sometimes called liqueur whiskies, are exactly the same product but matured for several years longer, for example, Dimple Haig, Johnny Walker Black Label, Dewar's Antiquary. These whiskies are drunk at the same strength as the everyday Scotch, i.e. 70° Sikes (40° OIML).

*Whisky liqueur* is whisky which has been sweetened and may have had flavouring ingredients added, for example, Drambuie, Glayva, Glen Mist.

*Scotch whisky production* is similar in many ways to the production of beer. They both start with the fermentation of *wort*, which is the sweet extract of malted *barley*. The quality of Scotch whisky is thought to be due to the quality of water which tumbles over granite rocks on its way to the distilleries. The smoke from the peat fires which imparts its flavour to the barley in the malting is also an important quality factor.

The latest product to be released from Scotch whisky distillers is white whisky, to counter the competition from colourless rums.

## UK law

Scotch whisky must be three years old before it can be sold in the UK and the label must show: the name and address of the bottler; the alcoholic strength; and the volume contained in the bottle.

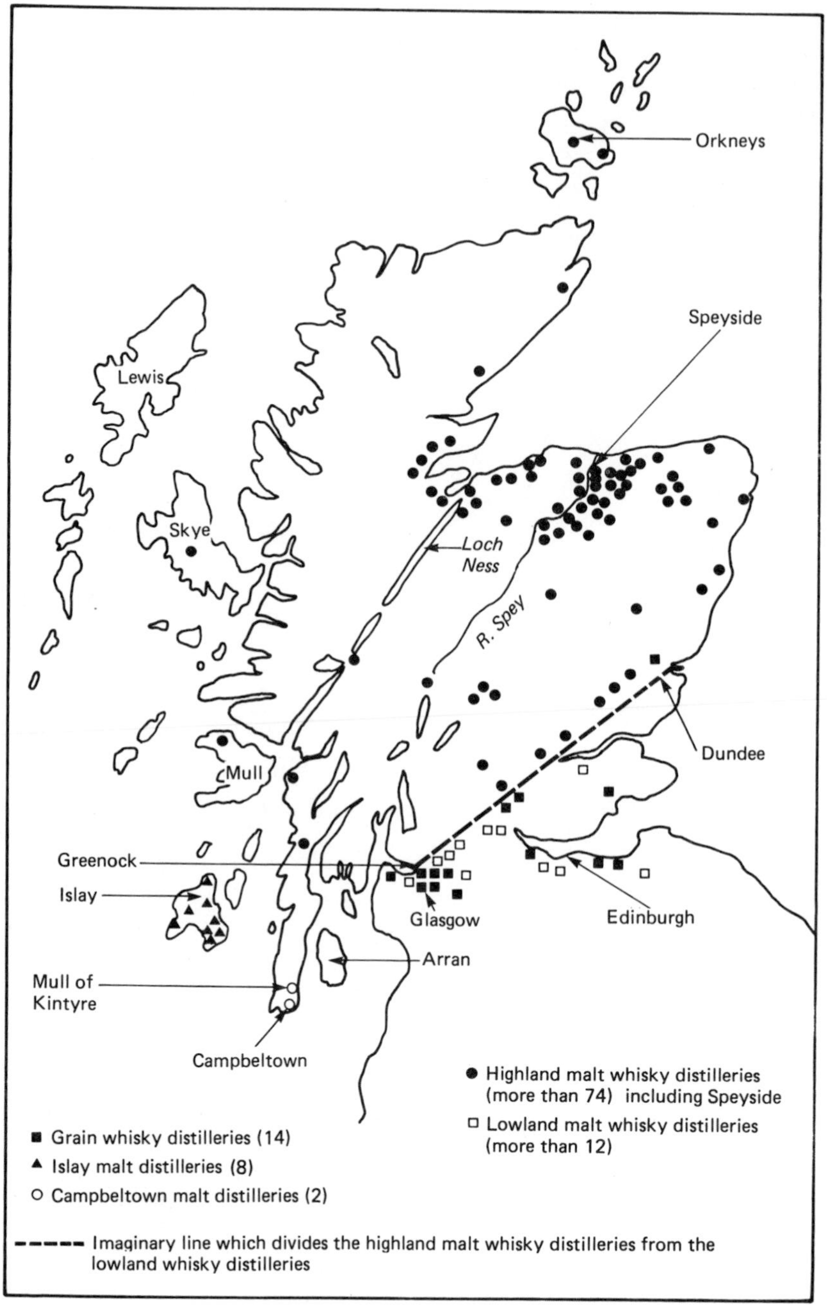

Orkneys
Speyside
Lewis
Skye
Loch Ness
R. Spey
Mull
Dundee
Greenock
Islay
Glasgow
Edinburgh
Arran
Mull of Kintyre
Campbeltown
■ Grain whisky distilleries (14)
▲ Islay malt distilleries (8)
○ Campbeltown malt distilleries (2)
● Highland malt whisky distilleries (more than 74) including Speyside
□ Lowland malt whisky distilleries (more than 12)
----- Imaginary line which divides the highland malt whisky distilleries from the lowland whisky distilleries


*The distilleries of Scotland*

## *Some well-known distilleries in Scotland*

*Single grain whisky*: Old Cameron Brig.

*Highland Malt whisky*
Skye—Talisker.
Orkney—Highland Park.
Speyside—Glenlivet, Glenfiddich, Strathisla, Dufftown.
Other highland malts—Dalmore, Glenmorangie.

*Islay malt whisky*: Lagavulin, Islay Mist, Laphroaig.
*Campbeltown malt whisky:* Springbank.

The predominance of whisky in the world markets owes its origin to the disastrous scourge *phylloxera*, which towards the end of the last century ruined the brandy vineyards of France. Scotch willingly filled the void and has maintained its lead in more than 160 countries in the world.

# Whiskey

### Irish whiskey

Most Irish whiskey sold today is made by distillation in pot stills, although some distillers do include a small amount of whiskey from patent stills.

The main differences between Irish and Scotch are:

1. Irish whiskey is distilled three times in pot stills, which are much larger than the Scottish stills.

2. The product, by Irish law, has to mature for five years before sale.

3. During the process of malting, the barley used for Irish whiskey does not come into contact with the peat smoke which is a feature of Scotch.

4. The Irish whiskey 'mash' is a mixture of malted barley (about 30 per cent), and unmalted cereals including barley, oats, wheat, and rye, while that used for Scotch malt whisky is entirely malted barley.

Many people on both sides of the Irish Sea believe that whiskey was born in Ireland and later introduced to Scotland. According to legend, St. Patrick taught the Irish the art of distillation 1,500 years ago.

Old Bush Mills, Jamesons, and John Power are examples of Irish whiskey.

### American whiskey

Settlers from Ireland and Scotland brought the art of making whiskey to America in the middle of the seventeenth century, and the spirit was first distilled to save the over-production of grain from deterioration.

Bourbon county, Kentucky, is the home of America's most famous whiskey. 'Old Crow' distillery was built by Dr James Crow in 1835 and national distillers still produce Old Crow whiskey by the pot-still process. All other bourbon is produced by patent-still methods.

The mash is made of at least 51 per cent maize, with wheat and barley. The maize, called 'corn' in the USA, is boiled in large pressure-cookers to release the starch. Bourbon is then matured in white oak casks which have been charred on the inside. Other famous American whiskey names include Jim Beam, Jack Daniels, Old Grandad and Four Roses.

### Canadian Whiskey

Canadian Club is the best known of the Canadian whiskies. They are all made from cereal grains with rye predominating, in patent stills, and they are matured in charred oak casks.

# Calvados

Calvados is a spirit made from apples or pears in Normandy, in northern France. It was first mentioned in a document in 1553, but had been made for several centuries before that date. The product of those days was probably bitter and bore very little resemblance to the drink we know today. Calvados is the name of a *departement* of Normandy and its name came from a Spanish galleon which was wrecked on the Normandy coast in 1588 on its way to England with King Philip's Armada. It was called the 'El Calvador'.

The apple juice for this spirit is fermented to give approximately 4 per cent alcohol. It is then distilled twice in a similar still to that used for cognac.

The *Pays d'Auge* is the heart of the region, producing the finest spirit which carries the Appellation contrôlée label. This means that the calvados spirit it contains comes only from the geographical region on the label, and it is protected internationally. The best of the Calvados may be matured for up to twenty-five years in wood.

There are ten districts called *Calvados Reglémentée*, which produce spirit less refined than that of the Pays d'Auge. It is roughly equivalent to VDQS in quality. The ordinary calvados is known as *Eau de Vie de Cidre* (or *Poire*) *de Normandie*. This is the cheapest type of calvados.

*Un trou Normand* literally means 'a Normandy hole' and refers to the practice of some diners of drinking a glass of calvados midway through the meal to aid digestion. Calvados is more usually drunk at the end of the meal from a glass warmed in the hands.

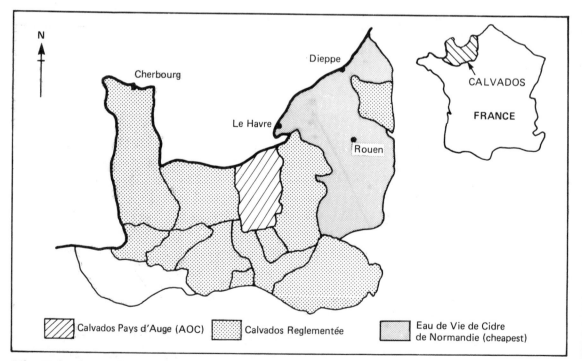

Key: Calvados Pays d'Auge (AOC) — Calvados Reglementée — Eau de Vie de Cidre de Normandie (cheapest)

*The Calvados region*

# Other Spirits

### Absinthe

A spirit which is illegal in most European countries due to the harmful effects of wormwood, which is one of the ingredients. It turns milky when water is added.

### Aquavit

A spirit made in *Scandinavia* from potatoes or grain and flavoured with herbs, predominantly caraway seeds. It should be served chilled, and is recommended to be drunk in one gulp.

### Arrack

A popular spirit made from the sap of *palm trees*. The trees are grooved like rubber trees to collect the sap. In some countries *rice* or *molasses* are added before fermentation. *Java*, *India*, *Ceylon* and *Jamaica* are the best-known producing countries.

### Bitters

These are spirits which have various aromatic flavours added. Some of the best-known examples are: *angostura, campari, fernet branca* and *underberg*. They have a very bitter flavour and are considered useful, (especially Fernet Branca) in curing hangovers and stomach upsets.

### Framboise

A fruit spirit distilled from raspberries in many parts of the world, but especially in *France* and Yugoslavia.

### Kirsch

This colourless spirit is produced in the Black Forest area of *Germany*, in *Austria* and *Switzerland*, and also in *Alsace* in France. It is made from cherries.

### Mirabelle

A colourless spirit made from plums in France.

### Ouzo

The name given to brandy made in *Greece* and flavoured with aromatic substances including *aniseed*. It turns milky white with water.

## Pernod

French *aniseed*-flavoured spirit which turns milky with water. The spirit contains herbs from the Jura mountains. When liquorice root is added to the blend, the resulting spirit is labelled Pernod Pastis.

## Poire William

This spirit is produced from *pears* in *Switzerland* and *France*.

## Poteen

An *illegally* distilled spirit made from *potatoes* around Connemara on the west coast of Ireland.

## Quetsch

Colourless spirit from *plums*, made in *Germany*, *France*, and the *Balkans*.

## Raki

Made in *Turkey* and *Eastern Europe* from *grain* or *potatoes* and flavoured with *aniseed* and *liquorice*. It turns milky with water.

## Sake

A Japanese spirit made from rice and served warm in porcelain cups.

## Schnapps

A spirit distilled from *potatoes* in *Germany* and *Holland* and usually flavoured with *caraway seeds*.

## Slivovitz

A *Yugoslavian* spirit made from plums which have fermented. It is twice distilled and left in cask for one year, when more plums are added. The spirit then matures for several years more.

## Tequila

Spirit distilled from the fermented juice of the *agave cactus* plant in Mexico. Traditionally it is drunk after a lick of salt and a squeeze of lime or lemon wedge.

## Vodka

A highly rectified *patent*-still spirit, originally from *Eastern Europe* but now made also in the *USA* and the *UK*. It is purified by being passed through *activated charcoal*, which removes most of the aroma and flavour.

# Speciality Coffees

Liqueur and spirit-based coffees are now very popular. While there should be no great difficulty in making them, a few simple rules should be observed in order to avoid a badly-made and unattractive beverage. The correct sequence for a successful and appetising drink is:

1 After the customer has decided which spirit or liqueur they would prefer in the coffee, a check should be written and taken to the bar or liqueur trolley. The duplicate copy is taken to the cashier. Another check, written on the waiter's food check-pad, must be made out to obtain coffee from the still-room.

2 Warm the glass, usually a goblet of 5 or $6\frac{2}{3}$ ozs. This may be done by pouring hot water into it from a clean jug and then back into the jug again.

3 Place the measure of spirit or liqueur into the warm glass. Some stylish restaurants flame a little of the chosen liquor in the goblet as a means of warming the glass.

4 Next, place a teaspoonful of sugar in the goblet, leaving the spoon in it so that the glass is less likely to crack at the next stage.

5 Pour hot black coffee into the goblet and stir until the sugar has dissolved. A space should be left at the top of the glass so that cream can be floated on top of the coffee.

6 Taking care that the coffee is not still revolving, gently pour unwhipped double cream over the back of the bowl of the teaspoon, which should be just touching the surface of the coffee. The collar of cream should be about a quarter of an inch thick and should contrast in colour with the black coffee underneath.

7 Present on a doily on a side-plate.

*Speciality coffee*

*Some favourite spirit and liqueur coffees include:*

Irish Coffee—Irish Whiskey.
Caribbean Coffee—rum.
Calypso Coffee—Tia Maria.
Balalaika Coffee—vodka.
Highland Coffee—Scotch malt whisky.
Monk's Coffee—Bénédictine.
Café Napoleon—Cognac brandy.
Café Royale—Cognac brandy.
Witch's Coffee—Strega.
Yorkshire Coffee—Brontë liqueur.
Gaucho's Coffee—tequila.
Kentucky Coffee—Southern Comfort.
Bonnie Prince Charlie's Coffee—Drambuie.

# Liqueurs

A liqueur is a *sweetened* and *flavoured* alcoholic beverage which is obtained by the distillation or infusion of aromatic and/or fruit substances with potable (drinkable) spirit.

Many of the well-known liqueurs were first made in the monasteries of Europe. The necessary herbs grew in the mountains near the home of the monks, who compounded the liqueurs to distribute as medicines on their travels around the village communities. Many of the herbs are known to have curative powers and income of the monasteries was largely derived from monies and goods received from satisfied patients. Liqueurs are acknowledged as *digestifs*, useful in preventing indigestion after a large meal.

Catherine de Medici, the queen of Henry II of France in the sixteenth century, introduced Italian cuisine and the use of liqueurs to the court of France.

## Manufacture

Liqueurs are based on spirits, with cane sugar used to sweeten them. Herbs, fruits, seeds, leaves, roots, etc. may be infused in water or spirit to extract the flavours. The extracts are added to the spirit, which may then have to be clarified.

Some liqueurs are made by the distillation of the main flavouring ingredient. In this case the resulting spirit may be artificially coloured as the distillate is colourless when it comes from the still.

Many of the herbs and seeds will not stand up to heat treatment, so the infusion method must be used. The resulting liqueur retains much of its original colour and may not need to be artificially coloured except in trace amounts.

### Service of liqueurs

Many restaurants have a trolley which contains a large selection of bottles of liqueurs with the appropriate glasses.

The effect of seeing the trolley beside their table is often sufficient to persuade the diner to order a drink in a way that a printed list could not do. The liqueur glass should be filled to just below the rim, so that it can be served without spilling. Hold the glass by the lower part when serving and place it to the right of the customer.

*A liqueur trolley*

# Herb Liqueurs

*Anisette*   Produced in Bordeaux by Marie Brizzard, it has an aniseed flavour.

*Aurum*   Golden Italian liqueur made from orange peel and herbs.

*Bénédictine*   Light amber liqueur made from forty herbs at Fécamp Abbey in Le Havre. The abbey itself was destroyed in the French Revolution but the secret recipe was saved. Bénédictine is reputed to be an effective cure for rheumatism.

143

*Brontë*   Popular Yorkshire liqueur in a distinctive pottery jar. It is based on brandy and flavoured with herbs.

*Centerbe*   Made in Italian Abruzzi mountains from one hundred herbs and brandy.

*Chartreuse Green*   The strongest of all liqueurs (96° Sikes). Made by monks of Carthusian Order at Grenoble, in the French Alps, from local herbs.

*Chartreuse Yellow*   (75° Sikes). Also made by the monks but sweeter and softer. Several imitations of Chartreuse exist.

*Cordial Médoc*   Red brandy-based liqueur made in Bordeaux, flavoured with old claret and herbs.

*Drambuie*   The oldest whisky liqueur. Secret recipe handed by Bonnie Prince Charlie to Mr Mackinnon, who helped him escape after the battle of Culloden in 1746. In Gaelic it means, 'drink that satisfies'.

*Galliano*   Golden yellow Italian liqueur in very tall thin bottle.

*Glayva*   Herb liqueur made in Scotland on a base of Scotch.

*Glen Mist*   Scotch whisky liqueur containing honey, herbs, and spices.

*Goldwasser*   Colourless or light-gold liqueur with flakes of floating gold-leaf and an aniseed and caraway flavour. Produced since 1598 in Danzig (but now in Berlin). There was a belief that gold prevented disease.

*Izzara*   Produced in green (strongest) and yellow, from herbs collected in the French Pyrenees and based on armagnac brandy.

*Kümmel*   Made in Holland and Germany for over four hundred years. It has a delicate pale green colour and is flavoured with caraway seeds, cumin, orris root and fennel.

*Menthe (Crème de)*   Mint-flavoured liqueur sold either as bright green or colourless. Freezomint is made by Cusenier in Paris.

*Monte Aguila*   Jamaican liqueur based on rum and flavoured with pimento.

*Palo*   Liqueur made in the Balearic islands, with a flavour of thyme.

*Sambuca*   Colourless Italian liqueur flavoured with liquorice. Served with a flaming coffee bean floating on the surface in some restaurants.

*Sapin d'Or*   Green liqueur in a bottle shaped and coloured like a log. It is flavoured with herbs from the Jura mountains in France.

*Senancole*   Yellow herb liqueur named after the river which flows near the Cistercian monastery in Provence where it is made. The monks gather the herbs and carefully guard the secrets of its manufacture.

*Strega*   Yellow Italian liqueur made from seventy herbs and bark. Legends say that it was first made by beautiful maidens dressed as witches, and according to tradition a man and a woman who drink it will never part.

*Trappistine*   Pale greeny-yellow liqueur based on armagnac, flavoured with herbs freshly gathered by Trappist monks.

*Vieille Cure*   Armagnac and cognac brandy is used with fifty aromatic herbs and roots. It is made in the Gironde area of Bordeaux.

# Fruit Liqueurs

*Ananas (Crème de)*   Pineapple liqueur on a rum spirit-base, from Holland and USA.

*Apricot Brandy*   Made in many countries, using apricots (often dried) and brandy.

*Bananes (Crème de)*   Ripe bananas macerated in spirit. Strong banana aroma.

*Blackberry Brandy*   Fully ripe blackberries steeped in brandy. Made in a number of countries but especially Poland and Germany.

*Cassis (Crème de)*   French liqueur from blackcurrants in eau-de-vie.

*Cherry Brandy*   Grant's Morella cherry brandy has been famous for over one hundred years using English cherries from Kent. De Kuyper also produce cherry brandy in Europe.

*Cherry Heering*   Danish cherry brandy produced by Peter Heering.

*Cointreau*   Made at Angers, in the Loire, from oranges and brandy.

*Curaçao*   A liqueur from the Dutch East Indies made from the peel of small bitter oranges. Made in several colours—orange, blue, green, etc.

*Forbidden Fruit*   Old American brandy-based liqueur made from Shaddock grapefruit with honey and orange. Sold in an attractive orb-shaped bottle, it is bright-red in colour.

*Fraises (Crème de)*   Made in the South of France from strawberries.

*Fraisia*   Italian strawberry liqueur with a brandy base.

*Framboises (Crème de)*   Fully ripe raspberries macerated in spirit in Holland and the South of France.

*Grand Marnier*   Orange-flavoured liqueur based on fine cognac brandy in the Cognac region. Two qualities are made, red label and yellow label, the yellow label being cheaper and preferred for kitchen use.

*Kirsch Peureux*   Sweet colourless French cherry liqueur which is quite different from kirsch spirit.

*Kiwi Fruit*   Green liqueur made in Holland from kiwi fruit and spirit.

*Mandarine (Crème de)*   Produced in Denmark, Holland and France from the dried peel of mandarin oranges with brandy.

*Mandarine Napoleon*   A fine example of a mandarin liqueur, from Belgium.

*Maraschino*   Colourless liqueur produced by distilling fermented maraschino cherries with the crushed kernels.

*Midori*   Japanese melon liqueur, bright-green in colour.

*Parfait Amour*   Violet or pink in colour with a delicate flavour of lemon peel and flower petals.

*Peach Brandy*   Made from peaches and brandy in several European countries.

*Southern Comfort*   Bourbon whiskey base (USA) with peach flavouring.

*Van Der Hum*   Literally meaning, 'what's his name', this is a South African liqueur made from small oranges and other secret ingredients.

# Other Liqueurs

After consideration of the two main groups of liqueurs, those which are herb flavoured and fruit flavoured, there remains an assortment of very fine liqueurs made from natural ingredients which are neither fruits nor herbs. While it could be argued that coffee and cocoa beans are fruits in the true sense, they would not readily be classed as such by most people.

### Coffee liqueurs

*Bahia*   Made in Brazil from coffee beans and local grain spirit.

*Kahlúa*   Danish fine quality liqueur from Mexican coffee beans and rum.

*Tia Maria*   Popular Jamaican product from local rum and coffee beans.

### Liqueurs containing flowers or twigs

*Edelweiss*   Italian flower liqueur containing sugared twigs.

*Fior D'Alpi*   Literally, 'flower of the alps'. An Italian sugared-twig liqueur.

### Chocolate flavoured liqueurs

*Cacao (Crème de)*   Made from Venezuelan cocoa beans and vegetable extracts.

*Hallgarten*   This company produces a popular range of 'Royal'

146

liqueurs: Royal Mint Chocolate, Royal Banana Chocolate, Royal Ginger Chocolate, Royal Raspberry Chocolate, Royal Cherry Chocolate, Royal Orange Chocolate, Royal Lemon Chocolate, Royal French Coffee Chocolate, Royal Apricot Chocolate, Royal Tangerine Chocolate, Royal Nut Chocolate, and Royal Fruit and Nut Chocolate.

### Whisky/cream liqueurs

*Bailey's Irish Cream*   Liqueur which includes Irish whiskey and cream.
*Carolans*   Irish whiskey and cream liqueur.
*Merlyn*   Liqueur made from cream and whisky from Wales.
*Atholl Brose*   Distilled oatmeal, honey, and cream, with malt whisky. (The Scotsman's breakfast distilled.)

### Egg liqueur

*Advocaat*   Low in alcohol, made from brandy, egg yolks and sugar. Produced in Holland by Bols. Warnink's Advocaat is also very popular.

### Nut and kernel liqueurs

*Amoretto di Sorono*   Italian liqueur made from apricot kernels.
*Noyau (Crème de)*   Strong French peach and apricot kernel liqueur.
*Malibu*   Coconut milk liqueur made in London.

### Ginger liqueur

*Ginger Brandy*   Brandy with the flavour of root-ginger.

# The Measurement of Alcoholic Strength

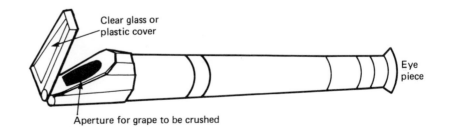

*A refractometer*

## A refractometer

Before fermentation takes place, the amount of *potential alcohol* can be measured using a *refractometer*. This instrument is used to assess the sugar content of the *must* (grape-juice) before the start of the vintage. A grape is crushed into the end of the refractometer, which is then held to the eye and pointed towards the sun or some other bright light. If the grapes are ready for harvest the scale inside the eye-piece will indicate this by showing the sugar level. If the scale shows a low level the harvest will be delayed.

## The OIML scale

Previously the Gay Lussac 'GL' scale, the *Organisation Internationale Météorologique Légale* scale is directly equal to the percentage of alcohol by volume. It is the universally accepted scale for the measurement of alcohol.

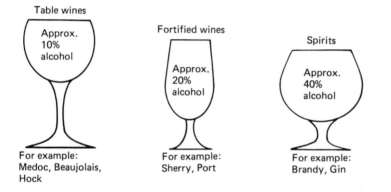

Table wines
Approx. 10% alcohol
For example: Medoc, Beaujolais, Hock

Fortified wines
Approx. 20% alcohol
For example: Sherry, Port

Spirits
Approx. 40% alcohol
For example: Brandy, Gin

## The Sikes scale

Bartholomew Sikes, a customs and excise officer, invented this scale, known as the *proof* scale, in the early nineteenth century. 'Proof' is a point on the scale. It is 100° Sikes and is the point at which the liquid would ignite if mixed with gunpowder and touched with a naked flame. Anything which did not ignite was termed *under proof*. If the liquid did burst into flame it was *over proof*. Proof was what the customs-men needed in order to convict smugglers, i.e. proof that it was brandy which they were smuggling into the country and not lesser stuff!

*Note* The alcohol strength of beers and ciders can vary between 4 per cent and 12 per cent.

Shown using three scales of measurement:

1. OIML (continent of Europe) scale
   range 0° – 100°
   Previously named Gay Lussac scale
2. Sikes Scale (United Kingdom)
   range 0° – 175.1°
   'Proof' is the point 100° on the Sikes Scale
3. American Scale (USA)
   range 0° – 200°

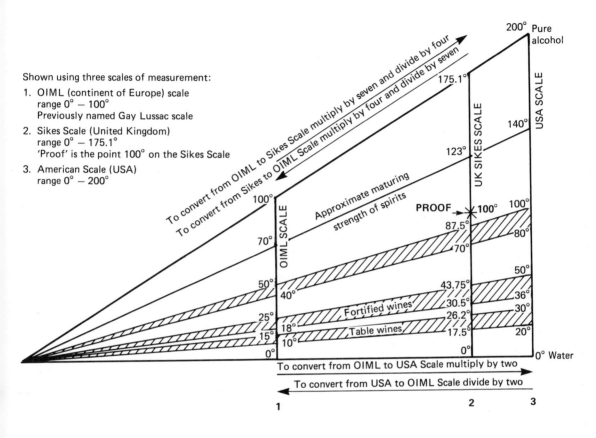

*Alcoholic strength*

# Part 9:

# Storage of Alcohol and Other Items

*Storage*
*Control*
*Tobacco*
*Cigars*

# Storage

### Bottled beer

Bottles of beer should be stored in clean conditions without extremes of temperature. Beer which is too cold will develop a *chill haze*. The sun's rays are harmful to beer so most brewers bottle their beer in dark bottles.

The life-expectancy of bottled beers can vary enormously. Brown ale has a shelf-life, when in excellent conditions, of about three weeks. Light ale will keep for about six weeks in reasonable surroundings. Stout, lager, and nips of strong ale have an expectation of about six months.

*All bottles* placed on the bar shelves should be wiped clean with a damp cloth and carefully arranged so that the bottles already on the shelves are pulled forward to make room for the newly requisitioned stock, which should be placed behind them. All bottle labels should face the front so that every shelf always has a presentable appearance.

### Draught beer

Mild and bitter beers may last for about four weeks but are best if sold within one week of delivery. Draught guinness has a slightly longer life, but the object of every cellar worker is to sell the casks and kegs as quickly as possible. Draught beer has a reputation for rapid deterioration if subjected to any sudden temperature change. Casks of beer which are left for several days half-sold quickly become unpalatable. It is important therefore to anticipate the quiet times so that a smaller cask can be used until the busy time comes round again. An even better solution would be to even-out the volume of trade by attracting in more business on the days which are normally slack.

Taking all the above facts into consideration it is in the best interests of the licensee to keep just over one week's supply of each item in stock. Deliveries are made on a weekly basis and it is inadvisable to have too much capital tied up in unsold liquor stock.

### Minerals

Minerals should be kept cool and stored in an upright position. When the winter is at its worst there is the possibility of minerals freezing if they are stored in unheated stores, which causes bottles to burst.

### Spirits

Spirits do not improve in bottle and, like beers, they do not like extremes of heat or cold. Brandy and rum are subject to haziness in very cold weather and must be very gently warmed to bring them back to clarity. Spirits are best stored upright to prevent the spirit coming into contact with the metal cap.

## Liqueurs

The shapely liqueur bottles make an attractive display and to some extent can sell themselves. They have a very long shelf-life out of the direct sunlight and can quickly be replaced. Only a small reserve stock is necessary.

## Wines

Bottles of wine should be stored (binned) on their sides, preferably in the dark. If a bottle of wine is stored in an upright position for long, the cork will dry out and shrink, and decay may set in. As with beer, it is best to avoid any sudden temperature changes or draughts. Allow for a free circulation of air around the wine-bins, with a space against the wall to avoid the accumulation of dust. Where space is restricted it is best to store white and rosé wines nearest to the floor, with the red wines nearest to the ceiling. This is because warm air rises. *Fortified wines* should be stored upright, vintage port being the exception to this rule. Bottles of vintage port should be binned on their sides, with the white splash of paint uppermost.

*A wine cellar*

## Maximum ages for wine

*Vintage champagne* may keep for up to *twenty years.*
*Vintage red* wines will keep from *forty* to *one hundred* years, depending upon the tannin content.
*Hock* is expected to stay in good condition for about *twenty* years.

*Moselle*
*Alsace* } are best drunk between *two* and *seven* years.
*Beaujolais*


## Temperatures

The ideal temperature for a beer cellar is 58°F (14°C).

Wines should be stored at a constant temperature of between 45°F (8°C) and 50°F (10°C).


## Tobacco

Cigarettes and cigars should be stored in a wooden cupboard at room temperature (65°F or 17°C). Worthwhile quantity discounts are given by cigarette firms. This is an important consideration when deciding how many to order. Once again, too much capital tied up in unsold stock is not good management.

Cigars are often packed in cedarwood boxes as this wood does not impart any unpleasant odours to the cigars.

**Note** *Remember that all storage areas must at all times be very clean and tidy—for reasons of hygiene and to facilitate efficient working.*


# Control

If a business is to thrive, the manager must ensure that an efficient set of control systems is followed. Staff are happier working in an environment where control is exercised firmly, and honest staff do not take exception to regular and systematic stock checks.

Alcoholic liquor must be recorded on arrival and checked against the original order in the *duplicate order book*. Empties and returns must be counted before they are taken away by the delivery staff. A *credit note* may be given by the van-driver or it may be sent by the company later. Credit notes are *red*. Deliveries are normally made on a weekly basis. Prices and cash additions must be carefully checked and entered in the *cellar ledger*. Where *bin-cards* are used, they must be updated daily with information about purchases and issues to departments.

*Requisitions* for cellar stocks are made out daily and passed to the cellar before 9.30 am. They must be signed by the person in charge of the department concerned. A duplicate copy is kept for use when the items are issued. In most establishments the cellar controller will deliver the liquor before opening-time to the lounge bar, public bar, dispense bar, restaurant, etc. A signature may be required for control purposes.

A *daily consumption sheet* is kept in the dispense bar, where the public have no access, and where issues are made to waiters and waitresses only. Control of stocks used is much more difficult in public, lounge, and cocktail bars, especially where mixed drinks are served. *Bar stock sheets* record the bottles received, but control is only possible by means of regular stock checks to deter pilfering and carelessness. An annual *stock-taking* is required by law for statutory record purposes, income tax etc., but most companies operate a monthly check. Spot checks are also a feature of bars, especially if a large number of staff is employed. Great care must be taken to ensure maximum security of liquor stocks by locking all doors, cupboards, and cabinets where alcohol or tobacco is stored.

Security of cash is poor in many hotels, but this need not be the case. Unusually large amounts of cash should not be kept on the premises, and a good quality *safe* in a secure location should be used for customer's safe deposits, cash floats, and takings.

*Keys* should be available only to senior trusted staff. *Closed circuit TV cameras* enable control staff to monitor all movements around areas where a security risk is identified. Careful selection of staff before appointment will help to minimise the absorption of dishonest staff into the organisation.

The issue of waiter's check-pads must be strictly controlled and a record kept of when and to whom the pads were issued. Checks should also be carefully controlled after use and married up with their duplicates to ensure that no 'smart' fraud is taking place.

### Tills

Advanced electronic tills have the facility to exercise control of cash and stocks and at the same time make the bar-person's job easier and speedier. The Sharp RZ 5700 is one of the most advanced 'intelligent' terminals. There are 114 positions on the splashproof keyboard to record the sales and adjust the stock position.

*The Sharp RZ 5700*

*The Sharp ER 1075*

The memory is such that many bar attendants can work on it at the same time. It gives a full itemization of sales and programmable print-outs of sales transaction details. Profit margins etc., are automatically calculated and control is the best yet devised. It can form part of a network of terminals with master and sub-masters. Organisations working on a smaller scale can still operate electronically with very little capital outlay. The machine illustrated (page 155) is an electronic cash register. This model is an ER 1075, which can be programmed to suit the needs of each individual business. The two-way digital display shows the amount of change to be given after the amount tendered has been entered. It can also be programmed to give a customer receipt. The time is printed on all transactions and the date changes automatically. The 'x' function on electronic tills is to print out the totals of groups or categories as programmed with the key in the 'x' position. The 'z' is for reading and resetting the totals and clearing the machine. Whichever type of machine is being used, all staff are shown how to use it properly and every machine has operating instructions which should be left under or near to the till.

Finally, remember to lock the restaurant till as electronic tills as well as teaspoons have been known to disappear!

# Tobacco

Almost half a million people smoke cigars every day in the UK. Owing to the anti-smoking publicity of recent years there has been a sharp decline in the number of people smoking cigarettes, but the appeal of cigars, which are considered to be less of a health hazard, has increased. A timely approach by the wine-waiter at the end of the meal can result in a sale. A well-presented display in the restaurant or bar can also help to improve cigar sales and turnover. Some restaurants have a small cigar list which is placed on the table in front of the guest, while other establishments wheel a cigar trolley to the table.

## Origins and history

Tobacco was probably first smoked two thousand years ago by the *Mayas*, an ancient South American civilization, as they worshipped their cloud-gods, imploring them to send rain. In 1492 Christopher Columbus sent men ashore in North America and they saw Indians smoking rolled-up leaves of aromatic plants, probably the 'pipe of peace'.

Smoking for pleasure did not start in Europe until 1556, when a sailor in Bristol 'did walk in the streets emitting smoke from his nostrils'; he managed to escape after a chase through the city streets. But Sir Walter Raleigh made smoking fashionable by introducing it to the court of Queen Elizabeth I in 1586. The pipes they used then were made of clay.

Tobacco had been grown commercially in *Brazil* since 1548 and in India (not a colony of England until 1763) from 1605. Plantations were established in the English colonies of *Virginia*, which sent home its first supply in 1613, and in *Jamaica*. By 1615 there were more than seven thousand shops in London selling tobacco. The first London coffee-house was opened in 1652, where intellectuals could pass away the time in serious conversation over mugs of coffee and a pipe or two of tobacco. During the Great Plague in 1665 boys at Eton were whipped if they did *not* smoke. Smoking is still considered by many people to be a defence against harmful bacteria. However, smoking can cause heart disease, bronchitis and other chest diseases; more than 30 000 people die each year in the UK from lung cancer.

*Licences* were first required to sell tobacco in the reign of King James I in the early seventeenth century. The first cigarettes were made in Spain and were called *papelettes*. *Briar* pipes, made from the roots of European *Erica* (heather), were first smoked in the early 1800s. Bristol, which was established in the fifteenth century, developed and expanded its influence because of the tobacco industry.

During the Crimean War the British troops smoked hand-made cigarettes with their Turkish and French allies. The smoking habit has continued to spread as a result of travel, and because of the impact of massive advertising since 1950.

# Cigars

The best quality cigar tobacco is grown in Havana, in Cuba. Other producers include: Sumatra, Java, Jamaica, Brazil and Cameroon. Cigar tobacco is also grown in the USA in the states of Connecticut (which specialises in tobacco grown in the shade, under cheesecloth, to preserve its colour for use as an outer wrapper leaf), Florida, Pennsylvania and Wisconsin. Other tobacco-producing countries, such as Zimbabwe, Nyasaland, Canada, India, Syria, Cyprus, and the North American states of Virginia, North and South Carolina, Georgia, Ohio, Florida, Kentucky, Tennessee and Louisiana, concentrate on cigarette and pipe tobacco. Florida produces all three types.

Black oriental-type tobacco, used for pipe-smoking and for cocktail cigarettes, which are sometimes offered with the sorbet course in banquet menus, is grown in the Balkan countries (Yugoslavia, Rumania, Bulgaria, Albania, Greece and Turkey) and is called Balkan Sobranie.

Cigars are made up of three parts, each using different quality leaves.

1 The *filler*: this is the centre, made up of blends of imperfect leaves of different tobaccos broken up.

2 The *binder*: one single strong leaf rolled around the filler to form what is known as 'the bunch'.

3 The *wrapper:* A single outer perfect leaf which is chosen for its appearance and texture.

## Sizes of cigars

There are six sizes of cigars which are, approximately: miniature (cigarette size); whiff (7.5 cm); cheroot (11.5 cm); panatella (13 cm); petite corona (13 cm, one round end); and corona (14.5 cm, one round end).

## Storage

After importation, tobacco is required to remain in the Customs and Excise controlled *bonded warehouse* for *two* years before it can be sold. The *duty* payable is an amount of cash which must be paid by the importer at the end of the two years when the tobacco is removed.

To maintain perfect condition, cigars should ideally be stored in *cedar-wood* boxes on slatted shelves made of wood which is unpainted and unvarnished, and well clear of any surface where condensation can occur. A free circulation of air, and a temperature of between 14°C and 17°C, is recommended. There must be no contamination by strong smells or perfume.

## Preparation of cigars for smoking

The cigar band should first be removed by the waiter at the customer's table by *opening* the band, and not by sliding the band along the cigar as this would damage the cigar wrapper. It would interfere with the drawing quality and make smoking impossible.

If the diner requires to have his cigar cut or pierced, the waiter should be competent and equipped to attend to it. Many types of cutters and piercers are manufactured. The one chosen should be sharp and used confidently on the round end of the cigar. Finally, most cigar smokers prefer to have their cigars lit with a *match,* not a lighter.

# Part 10:

# Customer Relations

*Personal Presentation*
*Merchandising*
*Wine Lists*
*Customer Contact*

# Personal Presentation

Lasting opinions are formed from first impressions when the diners walk into the establishment. The atmosphere and decor should create a feeling of comfort and luxury. To be greeted pleasantly and with *good humour* is very reassuring, especially in a strange environment. The appearance of the staff, with *smart attire* and *personal grooming,* gives immediate confidence that the service given will also be of a high standard.

All staff clothes should be well pressed and of a proper fit. Each business has its own rules about uniforms. In some cases staff are provided with properly laundered clothing, while others are more informal. But every employer who takes a *pride* in their enterprise will expect the staff to dress smartly, with clean hands, finger nails, and well-styled hair. Extremes of fashion usually restrict the job opportunities available. The service staff should not be the centre of attraction but should quietly blend in with the surroundings. Heavy make-up should be avoided and jewellery either non-existent or restricted to a minimum.

Good *deportment* gives confidence and body language is important. Front-of-house staff should display an upright posture and all movements should be purposeful and positive. Lounging and leaning, chewing gum, sitting around, and generally negative attitudes, do nothing to help to sell the products and services available.

*Speech* is an immediate and vital method of communication. Moods and temperamental outbursts by food and beverage workers can lose good customers. The tone of voice, the speed of speech, as well as the pitch and volume, can all make the waiter or bar-person sound disagreeable. Every effort should be made to improve vocabulary and the utmost discretion should be used to avoid words and phrases which might give offence to customers. Bad language and crude expressions do nothing to enhance the image of the person using them or the establishment to which they belong. Staff should be *articulate* and should pronounce their words clearly so as not to be misunderstood.

Personal attitudes and behaviour are usually acquired at a very early age. The hospitality and service industries require people who are able to demonstrate *courtesy* and *civility* at all times, and *tactfulness* on occasions when disagreements or arguments arise, or when you have information about events or people which it is wiser to keep to yourself. You may have to exercise great *patience* in dealing with people who continually complain, or with whom you find it difficult to communicate. Great *sensitivity* is needed, especially in establishments where guests are from abroad and where language barriers may prove to be a handicap to good communication. The effect of social factors in a multi-racial society requires from the staff an awareness of separate cultural differences, and an acceptance and understanding of the habits and traditions of other religions and races. Good humour and a pleasant manner help to break down barriers and make communication easier.

Formal *qualifications* for the food and beverage service industries, whether gained in colleges or in industry, all help to develop the individual's *self-confidence*. Experience increases the ability to react in the most acceptable way to whatever problem arises.

Staff must remain *polite* at all times, even when provoked, and they must not allow their temper to show. The customer is definitely *not* always right, *but* as far as possible he must be allowed to think that he is!

*Punctuality* and *reliability* are great assets, as is the ability to organise yourself before service, so that when the doors open and the first guests arrive, you have everything in place and do not appear disorganised and flustered. At all times you must be *alert* and *aware* of the needs of your customers. *Anticipate* the moment when you can re-fill the wine glasses, or produce the matches at the appropriate time when the cigar needs to be lit. Attention to such details leads to consumer satisfaction and may be just the final touch which is needed to ensure repeat business. Each diner, whether a regular or a chance caller, must be made to feel at all times thay they are the focus of your attention.

The importance of *team-work* cannot be overstated. A pleasant atmosphere between you and your colleagues will reflect itself around the tables and in your bar. A sense of *calm* will prevail. A willingness to help a fellow-worker who is at some time under pressure, or who is unwell, will be amply repaid when you yourself need help.

Your supervisors need a *willing* team, capable of following directions and obeying without dissent any instruction which is given. Management must be confident that you are able to work without direct supervision and that in their absence they can rely upon your ability and judgement to continue the service smoothly. When your work is criticised by your section leader, you must accept the criticism cheerfully as part of your experience and, learning from the occasion, endeavour not to allow the same situation to occur again. Even a reprimand, if accepted in the right spirit, can form a good bond between your supervisor and yourself.

Always treat your assistants, junior staff, cleaners and delivery van-drivers with *understanding*. Give them whatever help you can by way of advice, remembering the people who helped you when you needed support. When giving instructions to assistants, do so in a kindly manner, ensuring that your information has been understood, and if it is not understood, take time to go over it clearly again, pointing out the problems which could arise and satisfying yourself that the commis is in no doubt about what he is to do.

A *smiling*, relaxed attitude to work, coupled with a willingness to make the maximum effort towards the improvement in the service, and the success of the business with infinite customer satisfaction, will inevitably lead to promotion for you and expansion for your company.

*Co-operation between departments* is essential for a happy work-force in every organisation. You must make every effort to end any unpleasantness which exists as each department is equally dependent on the other.

# Merchandising

Most diners are cautious or even slightly suspicious when they enter a strange bar or restaurant. Many establishments do not take advantage of the opportunities which exist to create good, lasting customer relationships—people can be seen to drift in and out of food and wine outlets without making any purchase. The atmosphere and general feeling upon entry, or the negative attitudes of staff, make an impression on potential buyers. Therefore, the first priority should be to gain the customers' confidence when they come in to the premises.

The success of the enterprise starts outside the building. A clean, crisp, well-tended exterior is an attraction to passers-by and, if they don't call in when they first pass, they will continue to wonder on subsequent occasions what your business has to offer inside.

Once inside, it is up to you to greet customers and make them welcome. Engage them in conversation if they are alone but, at the same time, never lose sight of the opportunity to make a sale. Always have two or three drinks as your specialities for the evening. Display effective sales material, such as tent cards or notices, to draw their attention to particular lines. These will be having their unseen effect on one customer while you are serving another. Silent selling methods are subtle but rewarding.

Staff must be well trained in merchandising skills and able to respond to any situation with confidence. They must have patience even with the most demanding guests. Customer satisfaction brings repeat business to the establishment and job satisfaction to the employee. So, start your working day looking forward to your dealings with the public and you will be guaranteed to maximise the spending potential which comes through the door. Your preparation will ensure that the restaurant or bar is presentable, with all the pre-service duties properly attended to, glassware polished to pristine brightness, clean linen in its place, and all the shelves stocked ready for the first customer.

It is important to gauge how much the individual is able to spend and to resist the temptation to reach the point of 'over-sell'. An ability to assess the guest's possible requirements is an asset for a bar-person or sommelier. A skilful reading of the customer's sales resistance and service requirement is closely bound to a good working knowledge of the products for sale. Positive selling is based on a detailed knowledge of the wine list and an imaginative attitude to promotional techniques, such as highlighting one product for special emphasis. Examples of this include promoting Beaujolais Nouveau on the third Thursday in November, or holding an Alsace evening with foods and wines from the region, or organising 'Witch's coffee' made with strega on Hallowe'en.

# Wine Lists

Wine lists are just one of several types of sales promotional material. They are often very large and elaborately decorated, when much smaller and cheaper versions would be more effective. Customers could then be encouraged to take away their copy, thus keeping that restaurant firmly in their mind. Personalised drip-mats on the bar and serviettes featuring your premises may take their place in someone's collection at home, bringing back to them memories of a pleasant evening and prompting them to go again.

Wine lists must be clean and presentable with no untidy alterations. The content of the list should be such that any visitor would be able to find on it a wine to suit every occasion and to accompany every food. Obviously there should be champagne for special celebrations, as well as cheaper sparkling wine for the less affluent diners. Several examples of red, white, and rosé wines, including some which are sweet, some medium, and some dry, would enable the diner to find the right wine to suit his food and mood. Some fine vintage wines should be featured to please the gourmet connoisseur.

Aperitifs and good dessert wines start and end the meal and are also found in those positions on the wine list. As with all fortified wines, they are priced by the glass and not by the bottle.

The order of listing differs by establishments. Since aperitifs are drunk before the meal it is reasonable to expect them to be on the first page. Thereafter it is usual to list the most expensive wines first on each page. Champagnes and sparkling wines are invariably found on the page after the aperitifs. Some lists give details of all the red wines, followed by the rosés, followed by the whites, listing the most expensive first under each colour. Other restaurants place the wines according to country and region, with the best quality areas at the front and the less expensive wines at the rear. In this case it is most probable that French wines would lead the list with Bordeaux, followed by Burgundy, Rhône, etc.; then Germany, followed by Italy and so on. There is, however, a number of famous eating houses whose wine lists are unconventional and which do not feature any of the main European regions.

*House wines* are chosen because they are inexpensive and can be sold by the glass. The partially empty bottle of wine does not deteriorate as quickly as fine wine and will possibly keep in good serving condition for about 72 hours. Wines by the glass are very profitable and many people eating alone might not want or be able to drink a whole bottle of wine. House wines are often sold in carafes.

*Bottle shapes* can increase liquor sales. Drinkers will order Chianti in the wicker flask, Brontë liqueur from the pottery jar, and Vieille Cure from the stained glass window bottle so that they can take the empty bottle home.

# Customer Contact

*Welcoming* guests is often overlooked. People just drift into the restaurant instead of being met by a smiling member of staff. A few phrases of pleasant conversation after a sincere, 'Good evening Sir/Madam' can help to relax and unwind even the most nervous visitor. If the customer is a regular then they should be addressed by name when first greeted. For the rest of the visit they should be called 'sir' or 'madam', as appropriate.

Introducing people can be a good way of increasing trade. A bartender can often include people in conversation who are at separate ends of the bar. Making people feel at ease is a positive attribute in a sommelier. For too long the wine-waiter has been seen by customers as a demonic intimidating character to be avoided. Diners must be given the freedom to select the wines of their own choice, no matter how unusual.

*Conversing* with customers should be encouraged, provided that they are not already engaged in conversation with someone else. Both the bartender and the wine-waiter should be on good terms with their regulars.

Telephone contact with the world outside your restaurant or bar can be a very valuable means of increasing business. Care should be taken with enquiries from the public so as to promote your employer's business by sounding enthusiastic and making use of every opportunity to encourage trade. A cheery, 'Good morning, King's Head Hotel, can I help you?' sets the tone when the customer first telephones with a query about prices or whatever. It is even better if hotel staff can use their own names, e.g., 'Jane speaking, can I help you?', after the name of the hotel.

*Compliments* from customers should be accepted gracefully and reported to the management, and also to the kitchen staff and the cleaners if they are included in the comments. Complimentary customers are very likely to return and will certainly speak highly to other prospective diners.

*Elderly* members of the community may not be able to react quite so quickly as younger folk, and it is always necessary to show tolerance and understanding. Staff should show an interest in the lives of customers, so helping to establish good relationships. The wealth of experience possessed by older customers can be of great benefit. It is better always to try to show an interest, even if the conversation in the bar seems boring.

*Children* need firm but friendly control. If they are encouraged by way of special menus, non-alcoholic cocktails, and a room full of interesting activities, the parents are more likely to frequent your premises.

*Handicapped* members of the public expect to be treated as far as possible in the same way as the other customers. As service staff you may find yourself in a position to help; for instance, to explain the content of the wine list to an unsighted visitor. A little thought would inspire you to place the wheelchair occupant on the side of the table away from the main thoroughfare.

*Complaints* must be dealt with promptly, so that customers are not lost forever. If the complaint is justified, it may be necessary to invite the customer back on another occasion. Most people who complain think that they are justified and that the customer is *always* right. You may have your own views but all complaints should be referred to the supervisor. If you are the cause of the upset, apologise and make every effort to learn from your mistake.

*Drunks* can be the cause of many problems. Although it is illegal to supply alcohol to a person who is drunk, the licensee is sometimes faced with the person who arrives already the worse for drink. Your first priority is to remove them from your premises as quickly as possible, so as not to inconvenience or embarrass other customers. Usually, drunks fall into four categories: the *happy* drunk, who causes no problems; the *sick* drunk, who is very unwelcome; the belligerent drunk, whose *fighting* behaviour can give the establishment a bad name, and deter valuable trade; and the drunk who literally *passes out*, taking up valuable potential sales space! Wherever possible drunks, and all those who are obviously 'over the limit', should be discouraged from driving a vehicle.

*Violence* in a bar or restaurant must be speedily quelled. Those responsible should be removed as quickly as possible, using the minimum of force. Staff should inform the management or supervisor immediately and ensure that the police are called, in the interests of public safety, if the fracas looks like getting out of hand.

Whenever an emergency occurs the staff must exercise great calm and presence of mind. If it is a fire, then remember always that life is more important than property. New staff should be made aware of the procedures to be followed in the event of fire.

*Bombs* are a fairly modern hazard in mainland UK hotels, but numerous terrorist organisations exist with many political objectives. If a suspicious package is found, the manager should be told immediately and the police informed. If the building needs to be evacuated, the staff would be expected to help to direct the guests calmly and quietly to a place of safety.

In the event of *customer illness* action taken by staff must be prompt, as a life could depend on your speedy reaction. If the illness is obviously serious, then no time must be lost in calling for an ambulance or doctor.

*Accidents* must always be recorded in the accident book. Effective first aid should be carried out wherever possible and the ambulance station alerted if necessary.

*Thefts* which may occur will cause an atmosphere of distrust, especially if alcohol is stolen. Efficient control systems will dissuade staff from helping themselves to stock. Remember to lock all areas where thefts might occur.

There should be a definite procedure to follow with regard to *loss of property*. If you find a camera, for example, under a restaurant chair, it ought to be handed to the manager or reception. Write down the name or description of the person who last sat on that chair, to help locate the owner. People often leave with the wrong umbrella or coat. If a loss is reported, write full details of date, time, description of article, owner's name, address, and telephone number, and hand it to reception.

Finally, *departure* can be almost as important as arrival. When customers leave the establishment they should either be shown to the door, or, if you are behind the bar, give them a polite wave and a smiling, 'Have a safe journey' or, Hope to see you soon, sir'. Hopefully you will.

# Part 11:

# The Law, Health and Safety

# Legal Aspects

**The Licensing Act 1961**   This introduced restaurant and residential licences, and for the first time allowed drinkers in a bar time for 'drinking up', during which time the service of drinks is illegal. 'Wet' and 'dry' counties came into existence in Wales. The *1964 Act* dealt with permitted hours and the sale of alcohol to children and young persons.

**The Food Act 1984**   This act has brought together the *Food and Drugs Acts 1955* to *1982*. Under the Act it is an offence to sell or to offer for sale food which is not of the nature, substance, and quality demanded by the buyer.

**The Trades Descriptions Act 1968**   Enforced by the local Weights and Measures department, this ensures that false descriptions are not applied to goods sold or services offered. Such goods and services must not be of a lower quality than is claimed on the label.

**Weights and Measures Act 1963**   This states that a notice must be prominently displayed indicating the measure used for the sale of whisky, gin, rum, and vodka in units of $\frac{1}{4}$, $\frac{1}{5}$, or $\frac{1}{6}$ of a gill. (A gill is $\frac{1}{4}$ pint.) Mixed drinks of three or more drinks are exempt. Draught beer and cider may be sold by retail in quantities of $\frac{1}{3}$ or $\frac{1}{2}$ pint or multiples of $\frac{1}{2}$ pint.

**Race Relations Act 1976**   This act makes it illegal to discriminate against a person on racial grounds, meaning colour, race, nationality, or ethnic origin. These groups must not be treated less favourably than other people in respect of applications for jobs, house-buying, tenancies, membership of clubs, and provision of goods, services or facilities. Equality of opportunity must be the same for all people.

**Sex Discrimination Act 1975**   It is unlawful to discriminate against a woman in employment, training, education or the provision of goods, facilities or services. She must not be treated less favourably than a man. Promotion, training, and transfer opportunities must be equal. It is an offence to publish advertisements discriminating by sex.

**Food Hygiene General Regulations 1970**   These concern the cleanliness of premises and utensils used in the business, the provision of adequate toilet and washing facilities, infectious diseases, temperature requirements, and protective clothing.

**Measures**   Wine sold in carafes or 'by the glass' is controlled by legislation which requires that a notice is displayed prominently showing how much wine per unit is served in that establishment.

**Price Marking (Food and Drink on Premises) Order 1979**   Prices of at least six wines must be prominently displayed where they will be seen by an intending customer before reaching the area of consumption. (Two whites, two reds, and two rosés if sold, but six in total.)

**Blood alcohol level**   It is an offence to drive or be in charge of a motor vehicle when under the influence of alcohol. The legal limit is 80mg of alcohol in 100ml of blood. This may also be expressed as 35 microgrammes of alcohol in 100 ml of breath.

**Young Persons**   Children *under the age of fourteen* must not be allowed in any bar. This does not apply to the children of the licensee or a child who is a resident. A child may also pass though a bar if it is the only convenient way to reach some other part of the premises. Young persons *between fourteen and sixteen* years of age may be allowed into a bar with an adult but may not purchase or consume alcohol. *After* the age of *sixteen* but *under eighteen* years young people may purchase tobacco or cigarette papers. They may also purchase and consume beer, porter, cider or perry, with a meal in a part of the premises set aside for the service of food and which is not a bar. Licensees and their staff must not 'knowingly' allow any person under the age of *eighteen* to purchase or consume alcohol in a bar on licensed premises. It is also an offence on the part of the young person to purchase or consume alcohol in a licensed bar.

**Drunks** It is an offence to permit drunkenness or quarrelsome behaviour on the premises. Neither a licensee nor his staff must sell alcohol to a drunken person or a person who is blacklisted by the courts as an habitual drunkard.

**Permitted Hours** Liquor must not be sold outside permitted hours. Extensions to permitted hours and occasional licences for weddings etc. may be applied for to the local licensing magistrates. Residents on licensed premises may purchase and consume alcohol at any time of the day or night if the licensee agrees to serve them. They may also entertain an unlimited number of bona fide friends to drinks so long as it is the resident who pays.

**The Licensing (Restaurant Meals) Act 1987** Bona fide restaurateurs may serve alcoholic drinks with 'substantial' meals every afternoon of the week with licensing justices' approval.

**Prostitution** A licensee must not knowingly harbour prostitutes, i.e. they must not be allowed to remain on the premises longer than is necessary to obtain reasonable refreshment.

**Gambling** Betting and the passing of betting slips on licensed premises is illegal. The playing of games of chance for money is also forbidden. Dominoes and cribbage for small stakes is allowed. Games of skill, such as billiards, darts, skittles or shove halfpenny may be played for higher stakes.

**Right of Entry** A police constable may enter licensed premises for the purpose of preventing or detecting any offence under the licensing act during permitted hours and for half an hour after any period of licensed hours. Weights and Measures officers also have the right of entry to licensed premises and, if necessary, seizure of goods.

**Licensee's Responsibility** To provide a pleasant drinking environment while observing a long list of laws which have been framed to protect the public in general.

**Adulteration of Products** It is an offence under the Food and Drugs Act 1955 to mix together lower grade wines with higher grade products and pass them off as of the higher quality. It is also illegal to dilute beers, wines, or spirits with water before sale.

**Sealed Measuring Instruments** These are available government stamped to dispense a pre-determined quantity of beer in sight of the customer. Similar sealed measures are available, called 'optics', which are used to dispense a measured quantity of wines and spirits. (An even more up-to-date electronic drinks dispenser, which can be used for stock control as well, is also available now.)

# Fire

The responsibility for the safety of premises, staff and customers from fire must be shared by all the members of staff. The manager must instruct and rehearse the employees in fire drill procedures, and make sure that they observe strict practices to prevent danger, in particular the following:

1　Combustible materials must be stored safely in a special place.
2　Fire-fighting equipment and alarms must be maintained and checked regularly.
3　External fire-escape staircases must be in a safe condition.
4　Fire exits must not be blocked.
5　Wiring and electrical appliances must be periodically tested.
6　Sufficient ashtrays should be provided.
7　Electrical and gas appliances should be switched off after use.
8　Plugs should be removed from sockets when not in use, with the exception of refrigeration, deep-freeze, and cooler equipment, and some electronic cash registers and computers.
9　Fire-fighting equipment should be conveniently positioned.
10　The spread of fire and smoke should be controlled by smoke-stop doors, remembering that smoke and flame rapidly spread upwards.
11　Emergency lighting should be in working order.
12　Signs must be prominently displayed indicating fire exit routes.
13　The fire alarm must be easily heard throughout the building.
14　Notices must be placed in all staff and guest bedrooms giving details of fire procedures.
15　All staff should know how to operate fire-fighting equipment.
16　The telephonist must alert the fire brigade immediately if fire breaks out.

Many older premises in the tourist industry have wiring which is a potential fire risk. Some furnishing fabrics and carpets are found to be positively dangerous and care should be taken to check with the suppliers when purchasing. Also, ceiling tiles and many paints and varnishes encourage the speedy spread of flames. Therefore, fire-fighting equipment *must* be within easy reach as it is the first few minutes which are vital—before the fire brigade arrives.

Kitchen fat fires, and fires started by flambé lamps being used too near to curtains, are a constant hazard. Alcohol, especially spirit, is very flammable and should be handled with care.

## Staff training

All staff should receive a personal copy of written fire instructions and at least two half-hour sessions of *verbal* instruction by a person competent in fire-fighting. These should be repeated at six-monthly intervals. Exercises in fire drill should be carried out once every six months to check evacuation times. Details of all training should be recorded and one person should be nominated to organise staff fire training and co-ordinate the actions of staff in the event of a fire.

## Fire fighting equipment

The *Fire Precautions Act 1971* is concerned with the safety of people who are inside buildings when fire breaks out. Fire certificates are issued to hotels and guest-houses which have carried out the necessary modifications to comply with the act. Smoke detectors, water sprinkler systems and heat detectors may be recommended by the local fire prevention officer. Extinguishers of various kinds all have their different uses and should be sited accordingly.

1 *Fire blankets* should be used to exclude the air from fires in confined vessels, e.g. fat fryers. Care should be taken to shield yourself with the blanket when approaching the fire. Fire blankets are now being made of glassfibre.

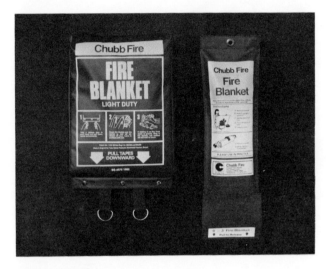

*A fire blanket*

2 *Water jet* extinguishers can only be used on paper, wood, textile and fabric fires. They must not be used on electrical or fat fires because water is a conductor of electricity, and oil and fat will float on the water, causing the fire to spread. They are also ineffective against gas fires. Water jet extinguishers are *red*.

*A water extinguisher*

3 *Carbon dioxide* extinguishers may be used on fires involving flammable liquids and gases, and those involving electrical equipment. But they must not be used in a confined space. $CO_2$ gas extinguishers are *black*.

*A carbon dioxide extinguisher*

4 *Foam* extinguishers are excellent for fat and inflammable liquid fires as well as fires of burning gases or organic solids. Foam extinguishers are *cream* in colour.

*A foam extinguisher*

172

5 *Dry powder* works effectively against all types of fire except blazing metals, for which there is a special extinguisher. Dry powder extinguishers are *blue*.

A *dry powder extinguisher*

6 *Halon* extinguishers are designed to deal with all types of fires, including flammable liquids and gases, and electrical hazards. They are ideally suited for motor vehicles, as well as general risk areas involving blazing oil and spirits. However, care must be exercised as the fumes given off are dangerous—especially in a confined space. Halon extinguishers are *green*.

A *halon extinguisher*

Whichever type of extinguisher you use, take care to read the instructions carefully at your leisure when there is no fire.

Smoke and heat detectors, and sprinkler systems, are fitted neatly on to the ceiling at regular intervals in bars, restaurants, and hotel corridors.

*A heat detector*

*A smoke detector*

*A water sprinkler system*

# Pests

### Moths

Moths cause great damage to curtains, blankets and other textiles, especially cotton and wool. Clothing and carpets should be inspected and sprayed if they are kept in storage for any length of time. Moth-proof preparations are readily available in the form of vapourising strips which can be hung in cupboards, etc. Moths often enter premises through open windows, attracted by the bright lights.

### Earwigs

Earwigs are so called because of the incorrect belief that this elongated insect likes to burrow down into human ears. It is no more likely to get into human ears than into any other small space. The worst problem is that they often fall into people's drinks from fresh flowers if glasses are left near vases. For this reason fresh flowers should be avoided on bars. Dahlias and chrysanthemums are especially favoured by earwigs.

### Black ants

Black ants may enter premises during the summer in search of food. If premises are infected, it is possible to open completely new packets of foodstuffs to find that the ants have already found their way inside. But a small quantity of 'Nippon' placed on a tinfoil dish is usually sufficient to kill several hundred ants, as it works by infecting one ant who carries the poison back to the nest, where others become infected.

### Wood-lice

Wood-lice prefer a damp habitat and keep themselves hidden. They feed on decaying wood. Special proprietary powders can be purchased to deal with any infestation.

## Spiders

Spiders are not a danger to health; in fact they may be beneficial in that they destroy other insects. They prefer dry warm rooms. The only reason for keeping down the spider population is that they are disliked by many people, both customers and staff.

## Cockroaches

Cockroaches are usually brought into the premises in containers of food. In common with many beetles they are nocturnal, keeping themselves hidden during the day. Cockroaches spoil food by their vomit and droppings. The treatment is the use of insecticide spray or powder in runs, ducts, clothing cupboards and other warm areas.

## House-flies

House-flies live on rotting organic materials, both animal and vegetable. All foodstuff debris should be removed from crevises, work-surfaces, wall and floors. Bins must be emptied regularly and lids should fit properly. Foods still fit to use must be placed quickly into correct storage. If foods are left uncovered, contamination is inevitable, owing to flies with hairy legs and bodies moving quickly from animal excreta on to food.

## Bluebottles

One female fly or bluebottle settles more than ten times every minute and carries on its body other creatures and bacteria hanging on for the ride. Eggs which she lays become maggots and more flies emerge. Treatment in food areas should be by electric ultra-violet. Avoid systems where the insect can go off and die on food.

## Silverfish

These are often found in warm, moist areas, such as kitchens and bathrooms and behind lifting wallpaper. They feed on carbohydrate materials and could infest flour products or books. Treatment should be with insecticide spray or powder in plaster cracks, and around plumbing installations.

### Cellar beetles and leather beetles

Both will be found in warm corners among dust, clothes, sacks, hair, etc. in dark areas. If treatment is used in cellar areas it must be odour-free in order to protect the draught beer. Cellar areas must be kept clean so as not to encourage infestation.

### Rodents

They are extremely dangerous to health. At the first sign of such company, precautions must be taken to block all possible entry points. Rodent control powder should be placed along runs. If not controlled, infestation will multiply due to the high reproductive capacity of female rodents. Rodent-control contractors will visit premises regularly if required. They are trained to recognise rodent presence by signs of gnawing on cabling, woodwork etc., and droppings.

# Cleaning

Scrupulous cleanliness is essential in *all* areas of the enterprise, not only in those parts which the customers see. Drinks are classified as foods for the purposes of law and all regulations concerning food hygiene apply equally.

Staff should be aware of methodical and effective cleaning systems, with floors, walls and furnishings regularly maintained. Efficient cleaning starts at the planning stage, with expert selection of the most appropriate surfaces and well-chosen fabrics and décor.

Equipment and materials for cleaning should be readily available when required and staff properly trained in the safe practical use of them. Careful control should be exercised in the storage and issue of cleaning materials. Regular servicing of large equipment should be a priority.

Staff training should be undertaken by a competent supervisor, as cloths and brushes, swabs and mops are generally misused by staff.

*Cloths* used for dusting should be washed frequently and used folded. 'High dusting' should be done at reasonable intervals, especially in food areas, to prevent the accumulation of dust on ledges, pipes, fittings, and high shelves. 'Low dusting' refers to areas within an arm's length of the worker and should be carried out daily. It is recommended that one area of the bar shelving should be systematically cleaned and polished every day, so that the total bar area is completely serviced every week. Linen cloths used for polishing glassware should be laundered regularly and not used for any other purpose.

*Brushes*—when areas have to be swept with a broom, this should be done before dusting takes place.

A 4 cm *paintbrush* may be kept behind the bar for brushing cigarette ends from the ashtrays into the rubbish bin. The ashtray may then be washed in hot soapy water, but quite separately from glassware or any other item.

*Bar-swabs* should be left soaking overnight in a mild bleach solution in a plastic bucket. Swabs which are not treated in this way give off that unpleasant stale 'beery' smell which should be avoided on licensed premises.

*Mops* are used for dry-mopping to remove marks from polished floor areas where sweeping is not effective. Dry-mopping restores the shine and gives a generally clean appearance. Wet-mopping is used to remove grease and stains from certain areas where sweeping is not enough to give a complete clean. The water used must be changed as often as possible to avoid a streaky finish.

*Vacuum cleaners* used by staff need to be sturdy models equipped with the necessary tools to clean carpets, curtains, and even baize-lined sideboard drawers thoroughly. A sufficient quantity of reserve dust bags and rings or belts should be kept by the supervisor.

*Glass-washing machinery* should be conveniently sited so that sterilised glassware can be quickly placed in position for the next day's trading. Staff should be made aware of the capability and capacity of the machine and a notice explaining its operation should be prominently displayed close by. Many modern machines rinse at a very high temperature, which causes the glassware to dry stainless and germ-free.

The maker's instructions with regard to liquid detergent and rinse-aid should be followed closely. Computerised automatic dispensers are provided with many modern glass-washers.


## Materials

Hot and cold running *water* should be present in every bar so that routine cleaning and glass-washing can take place. Double stainless steel sinks with two draining boards are necessary where manual glass-washing is to take place. Glasses should first be washed singly in a sink of hot water containing liquid detergent, and then rinsed in the second sink containing clean hot water only. Glasses should never be left in the water in the sink as this could cause an accident.

*Soaps* and *detergents* should be odourless and staff should pay careful attention to the quantities required for each purpose. The equipment which is to be used for the dispensing of beer must not be cleaned with soaps or detergents. Only proprietary pump and pipe-cleaning powders in solution should be used for the *weekly* beer pipe-line cleaning exercise. Beer taps should be placed in clean hot water for an hour or so then removed and placed in a clean lidded box or cupboard until required.

*Disinfectants* with strong odour can cause draught beer to go out of condition. It is best to avoid keeping them in the beer cellar.

*Abrasives* may be needed to remove obstinate stains from hard surfaces. A damp cloth should be used with abrasive powder.

*Solvents* are used for stain removal or cleaning grease or polish from certain surfaces. They have powerful fumes and are inflammable. Great care should be taken to follow the manufacturer's instructions as most solvents are also toxic, addictive, and may damage the skin.

*Polishes* are used to protect clean surfaces, mainly furniture, floors, and metals. Metal polish should be applied with a small cloth or polish applicator. The dried polish should be removed with a soft dry cloth. A soft brush is ideal for crevices or elaborate ornamental designs on punch-bowls etc. Metal items which are to be used with food should be carefully washed after cleaning.

*Furniture polish* may be of wax, cream, liquid, or silicone spray. The best effect is achieved if polish is used lightly on a clean dry area. Highly perfumed polishes should be avoided in the restaurant and bar.

*Floor polish* leaves a smooth shiny wax surface. The polish may be solvent-based or a water-based emulsion. The latter must not be used on porous floors because of its water content, unless the floors have been treated with a seal.

*Bleach*—chloride of lime is a bleach from which a mild solution may be made to clean the cellar floor and for using to soak the bar-swabs overnight. It has a sweet clean smell and does not harm the beer.

**Note** *Regular cleaning systems discourage infestation by vermin.*

# Problems of Alcohol

People employed in the *catering* and *drinks* industry are subject to far greater risks of alcohol-related problems than the average citizen. Statistics showing comparisons of deaths from *cirrhosis of the liver* list the occupational groups in the following order (using alcohol × 1 as the norm):

| | |
|---|---|
| Publicans and innkeepers | × 15.7 |
| Deck and engineering officers | × 7.8 |
| Barmen/barmaids | × 6.3 |
| Deck and engine-room ratings/boatmen | × 6.3 |
| Fishermen | × 5.9 |
| Boarding-house keepers/hotel managers | × 5.6 |
| Finance agents/insurance brokers | × 3.9 |
| Restaurateurs | × 3.8 |
| Lorry driver's mates/van guards | × 3.8 |
| Cooks | × 3.2 |
| Shunters and points men | × 3.2 |
| Authors and journalists | × 3.1 |
| Medical practitioners | × 3.1 |

People working in five of the above high-risk occupations have direct access to alcohol in their workplace. It is therefore necessary to exercise restraint and moderate drinking habits. Apart from the hazardous physical effects of alcohol, it is estimated that 500,000 people in England and Wales have a serious drink problem. In Scotland the proportion is thought to be even higher. The problem of alcohol dependency is indirectly the problem of their families and workmates also. A disturbing survey, carried out for the Medical Council on Alcoholism, found that even among thirteen to sixteen year olds, about one-third interviewed said that they had been slightly or very drunk more than once in the year! Alcohol consumption statistics show the UK lying twenty-fourth in the list of countries, with France, Luxemburg and Spain heading the drinking table.

## Alcoholism

An adequate definition of the condition is as follows: 'Drinking which continually or repeatedly interferes with the employee's work performance or normal social adjustment at work, or causes financial difficulties, or problems in relationships with family and friends, and where the drinker is not in control of his drinking.'

When taken in moderation alcohol is harmless, gives pleasure, and may even be beneficial. It is impossible to prescribe the limits beyond which drunkenness will occur. The age, weight, sex, state of health, and experience of alcohol, will all contribute to the effects of the intake. The results will also be slower if food is consumed rather than when drinking on an empty stomach, when 80 per cent will be absorbed into the bloodstream in forty-five minutes. Food activity in the stomach and intestines slows down the absorption of the alcohol and drunkenness is therefore delayed.

Whenever families meet together at weddings, or when people have something to celebrate, bottles are opened and corks popped. Alcohol has a socialising effect on the drinker, as it reduces the activity in the part of the brain which makes people shy or inhibited, which enables them to enjoy the event that much more.

The following drinks contain approximately equal amounts of alcohol: one single measure of spirit; one glass of fortified wine; one glass of table wine; one half-pint of beer. Each of these is considered as one unit of alcohol. It is advisable for a man to limit his regular drinking to six units each day. Females should restrict their alcohol intake to four units, owing to their smaller build. Women also have a higher proportion of body fat than men, leaving less tissue for the alcohol absorption. A further hazard concerning alcohol and women is that alcohol is extremely harmful to the unborn child, especially in the first four months of pregnancy.

Alcohol is blamed for much of the vandalism, fire, crimes of violence and cases of wife and child abuse that occur, as well as time lost at work through absenteeism.

## Legislation

The connection between excess drinking and driving has long been known and, in order to protect the public from itself, it has been necessary to introduce a level beyond which it is illegal to be in control of a motor-vehicle. The limit has been set at 80 mg of alcohol per 100 ml of blood; this may be expressed as 35 microgrammes of alcohol in 100 ml of breath. The police have the authority to make random checks of every driver on a given stretch of road.

Accident statistics show that one-third of all drivers killed in road accidents in the UK have alcohol in their blood in excess of the legal limit. The deaths during the time between 10.00 pm and 4.00 am show a staggering two-thirds who would have failed the breath test. Fridays and Saturdays, when people are out socialising and drinking, show the highest figures for road casualties.

Road accidents are the second highest cause of death, after cancer, in people between the ages of one and forty-five. Many people are of the misguided opinion that they 'drive better' after a drink or two, but in fact the chances of having an accident, due to carelessness or slowed reactions, increase with every unit of alcohol.

*Young persons* are more susceptible to alcohol than older people. It is for this reason that laws have been made to protect them:

1 Children under fourteen years of age may not be allowed in a bar or licensed premises except when passing through (e.g. to a toilet or stairs). Children of residents or the licensee are allowed in the bar.

2 Persons between fourteen and sixteen years may be in the bar with an adult but must not drink alcohol or be served with it.

3 Between sixteen and eighteen years of age, the customer may drink beer, cider, or perry with a meal, provided that it is served in a room which serves mainly food and is not a bar.

4 Persons under the age of eighteen must not be served with alcohol in a bar or off-licence and must not drink alcohol in a bar. They must not be employed in bars during permitted hours.

# Lifting

Many of the tasks which have to be performed by licensees, cellar-men, and others employed in the hotel industry, involve lifting and carrying heavy loads. The human body responds fairly well to reasonable situations, but it is necessary to avoid causing undue stresses and strains by incorrect handling of heavy weights.

The worker should consider the construction of the spinal column and the likely effect of jerky and irregular lifting jobs. Correct balance and careful timing are essential to avoid permanent injury to the spine, knees, neck, or elbows. Statistics show that many more working days are lost in British industry as a result of injuries to the back than from any other single cause. Such injuries are exceedingly painful and often could be avoided. Carelessly rushing down the cellar steps to change a cask, while customers are waiting in the bar, or hastily snatching up a crate of siphons with scant regard for the after-effects, can lead to much discomfort later.

*Picking up a case of wine*

*Lifting a case of wine*

### Simple rules for lifting

Clear all obstacles out of your way. Take care not to collide with colleagues. Gloves give protection from sharp edges. Think about the lift before you make it and try not to complicate the lifting process. 1) Keep spine straight. 2) Bend your knees and let your legs take the strain. 3) Arms should be straight and near body. 4) Use two hands to give even balance. 5) Consider the centre of gravity of the load. 6) Avoid snatching or sudden twisting. 7) Lift one case at a time to avoid unnecessary strain.

*Carrying a case of wine*

# Health and Safety

*The Health and Safety at Work Act* was aimed to increase the awareness of health and safety among managers and staff. It embraces all previous legislation and now covers *all* employers and employees except private domestic staff. Employers are also responsible for members of the public, or contractors, working inside or outside the premises.

The employer must ensure that *machinery*, *plant*, and *services* are in a *safe condition* and *properly maintained*. A reasonable working *temperature* is expected and sufficient provision for adequate *washing*, *sanitation* and *first-aid* facilities must be made. Where necesary, *protective clothing* should be provided and *fire-fighting equipment* should be conveniently sited. *Storage* and *handling* of materials and equipment must carry no risk to health or danger of injury. Employers must make sure their *staff* are *informed* and given reasonable *training*. The premises must be safe, with acceptable means of *access* and *exit*. Notice must be brought to all employees showing the *management's written statement* of general policy on health and safety. *Consultations* must take place with representatives from the *workers* about the arrangements.

Employees are expected to co-operate over matters of health and safety, taking all reasonable care for their *own* health and safety and that of *anyone else* who may be affected by them. Employees must not interfere with equipment provided for health and safety.

## Accident records

A record must be kept of every accident, however slight, involving personal injury. The record will be needed in the event of a claim being made against the company. It is also useful when analysing accidents and identifying their cause to prevent a recurrance. Every accident and its cause can be used to reinforce the safety rules at subsequent training sessions.

## Accidents

Accidents may happen because of human carelessness, bad behaviour, improper dress, lack of experience, lack of training, lack of supervision, fatigue, drinking too much alcohol, or drug abuse. Environmental causes may include faulty or unguarded machinery or tools, poor ventilation, bad lighting, dirty or overcrowded work-places, unsafe premises or dangerous surfaces.

*When an accident occurs*, attend first to the injured person, and if necessary call the ambulance, doctor, or company first-aid official. Switch off any machinery involved to prevent further injury. Inform the manager or person in charge, then you or they must obtain full details of the event and complete the *accident report*.

**Note** *the final level of responsibility is that of every individual worker.*

# Electric Shock

Electric current can travel widely through the body. It seals off blood vessels and may injure nerve and muscle fibre in its path. Breathing and blood circulation may be affected. The damage to the body is much more serious if the skin is in contact with water or metal as they are both good conductors of electricity. If the victim is 'earthed', by being in contact with metal pipes, the effects are much worse.

Because of the alternating current, the person touching the source of the electricity is often unable to release his hold on the object causing the shock. You must not touch the injured person becuse of the danger of you being electrocuted also.

If you find a person who has obviously suffered an electrical accident, your first action should be to switch off the current immediately or to pull out the plug. If it is difficult to reach the plug, it may be possible to pull the cord sharply, to wrench the plug from its socket. An alternative is to find something which is dry and does not conduct electricity, such as a wooden broom, or even a non-metal stool or chair. This can be used to pull the casualty away from his contact. Dry footwear may enable you to push the injured person sharply to disconnect him from the power.

In serious cases it may be necessary to give mouth-to-mouth or heart-lung resuscitation to revive the person. People injured by electrocution may appear to be dead when in fact their lives could be saved by prompt first-aid attention. The 'recovery' position illustrated is used to allow the person to regain normal easy breathing, but if the victim is not breathing, then mouth-to-mouth resuscitation may be needed. The technique is:

1 Lay the patient on his back.
2 Tilt his head back by placing one hand on his brow.
3 Hold his nostrils together with your thumb and forefinger.

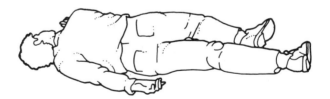

*The recovery position*

4 Take a deep breath and place your open mouth over the casualty's mouth while supporting his chin with the other hand.
5 Blow gently; this should cause the person's chest to rise.
6 If the chest does not rise, try again.
7 Take your mouth away from his, and wait for the chest to fall.
8 Repeat this process every five seconds until he starts to breathe or until another helper can take over.

If the casualty has no pulse or hearbeat it may mean that he is dead. But, after clearing the air passages and inflating the lungs twice, it may be possible to re-start the heart by squeezing it between the spine and the breast-bone.

## Heart-lung resuscitation

1 Place the 'heel' of one hand over the breast-bone, just above where the ribs meet.

2 Place your other hand over the first.

3 Press down vertically on the breastbone, with a smooth but firm movement.

4 Fifteen heart compressions should be given (at a rate of 80 per minute), followed by two lung inflations; repeat the cycle (15 compressions to 2 inflations).

5 Check the pulse after a minute and then after every three minutes, working until help arrives.

6 Try to work with urgency and without panic. It is important to restore ventilation of the lungs and circulation of the blood within minutes to revive the victim successfully.

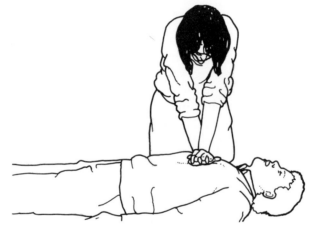

*Heart-lung resuscitation*

# Hazards

The following hazards could cause accidents in bars, cellars and restaurants and must be avoided wherever possible:

1 Faulty electrical equipment, including over-loading of power points, and poorly maintained wiring and appliances.

2 Electrical wiring placed under carpets.

3 Connecting a $CO_2$ cylinder directly to a beer keg without a reducing valve in position between the two.

4 Casks which are not properly controlled or secure when being delivered and lowered into the cellar.

5 Attempting to carry loads which are too heavy.

6 Uneven floor surfaces, especially in cellars and at delivery access points.

7 Slippery floor surfaces in service and storage areas.

8 Badly worn or torn carpets which can cause accidents to customers or staff.

9 Heavy items stored on high shelves.

10 Cleaning materials, such as bleach, being allowed to contaminate foodstuffs.

11 Lights not turned on early enough in public and working areas.

12 Protruding nails or splinters on restuarant or bar chairs.

13 Knives not kept clean and sharp.

14 Careless opening of sparkling wine without control of the cork.

15 Clumsy handling of glassware, e.g. trying to carry too many at once.

16 Glasses left in washing-up water in the sink.

**Note** Accidents are less likely to occur when you are alert and wide awake. Remember to inform your supervisor of any accident, even a small one, and make the necessary entry in the accident book.

# Conclusion

Opportunities for travel and adventure are enormous in the hotel, catering, and leisure industry. It is largely a matter of choice—catering for scientific expeditions, or working on an oil-rig, might not be the choice of every student leaving college. But fairly speedy promotion paths exist for the person with flair and determination in most sectors of the industry.

Make up your mind which aspect of the business pleases you most and set about achieving your objectives, such as:

1 Developing your own personal and social skills until you feel confident in any inter-personal relationship.

2 Studying hard to acquire as many qualifications as possible.

3 Cultivating as many contacts as you are able who would be willing to give you a reference when the need arises.

4 Varying your own work experience into a wide range of part-time activities while you are at college.

5 Reading widely around the subject areas which might be of use to you later.

6 Gleaning and storing as much information and practical expertise as you can from your lecturers or supervisors while at college or at work.

7 Visiting as many establishments as possible which you think would provide the kind of environment in which you would like to work.

8 Joining as many relevant organisations as you can afford as a student member.

When the time comes for you to start applying for jobs, write to the company concerned in a neat and legible hand. Enclose your Curriculum Vitae (CV), which is a picture in words of you and your achievements so far. It is always more impressive if a CV is typed. List on your CV all the establishments in which you have worked, even if it was for a short period only.

When you are called for interview remember to:

*Arrive on time, never late, and not more than fifteen minutes early.
*Dress appropriately. If you dress smartly the employer's first impression will be of a person whose care in appearance is likely to be reflected in their approach to work. (Extremes of fashion are unlikely to win you an appointment, however.)
*Answer questions confidently and politely.
*Show enthusiasm for the position for which you have applied and an interest in the company or organisation.
*Be prepared for the question 'Why would you like to work for this company?'
*Thank the interviewer even if you were not appointed.
*Learn all you can and use the experience for your next interview.

To close, I wish you good luck in your chosen career and I hope you will be able to maximise your sales and your abilities.

# Index

pergolas, 81
permitted hours, 169
Pernod, 140
perry, 123
personal presentation, 160
pests, 175
Petite Champagne, 131
pétillant, 30
phylloxera vastatrix, 10, 36, 40, 46, 137
Piedmont, 34
Pineau des Charentes, 84
Pinot Blanc, 24
Pinot Gris, 24
Pinot Meunier, 13
Pinot Noir, 13, 21
pipe, 76
Poire William, 140
Pomerol, 19
port, 69, 76, 84, 86
Portugal, 38
poteen, 140
pot still, 126
Pouilly Blanc Fumé, 26
Pouilly-Fuissé, 21, 27
pouring wine, 58, 62
Prädikat, 32
Premières Côtes de Bordeaux, 19
Premièrs Grands Crus Classés, 19
premium wines, 47
presses, 11
price marking order, 168
Priestley, Joseph, 125
prohibition, 130
Provence, 13, 29
pudding stones, 22
Puerto de Santa Maria, 78
puncheon, 135
punt, 62
Punt e Mes, 82
Puttonyok, 49

Qualitätswein, 71
QbA, 71
QmP, 71
Questch, 140
quinta, 76

race relations, 168
racking, 11
rainwater, 82
Raki, 140
Raleigh, Sir Walter, 41
Rasteau, 22
rayas, 78, 79

rebêche, 15
refractometer, 147
rémuage, 15
reserva, 71
residential drinkers, 100
Retsina, 52
Revolution, French, 20
Rheinhessen, 33
Rheingau, 33
Rheinphalz, 33
Rhône, 13, 22, 23
Riebeeck, Jan Van, 42
Riesling, 24, 33
right of entry, 169
Rioja, 36
Robertson, 43
Rolin, Nicolas, 21
Rossi, Fred, 41
Rothschilde, Baron Philippe, 52
Rousette grape, 30
Roussillon, 28
ruby port, 76
rum, 70, 133
rum verschnitt, 133
Rumania, 52
Rutherglen, 44

Ste Croix du Mont, 19
St Emilion, 19
St Joseph, 22
St Nicolas de Bourgueil, 27
St Peray, 22
Ste Macaire, 19
Sake, 140
Salisbury-Jones, Guy, 50
Salmanazar, 17
Sancerre, 26
sangria, 38
San Lucar de Barrameda, 78
San Sadurni de Noya, 37
Saumur, 26
Sauvignon, 19
Sauternes, 10, 19
Savoie, 13, 30
schistous, 76
schloss, 71
Schluck, 51
Schnappes, 140
Scotch, 70, 135
sec, 71
secco, 71
Sekt, 32
Semillon, 19
Sercial, 81, 86
serving wine, 54